On Bellow's Planet

On Bellow's Planet

Readings from the Dark Side

Jonathan Wilson

Rutherford ● Madison ● Teaneck
Fairleigh Dickinson University Press
London and Toronto: Associated University Presses

© 1985 by Associated University Presses, Inc.

Associated University Presses
440 Forsgate Drive
Cranbury, NJ 08512

Associated University Presses
25 Sicilian Avenue
London WC1A 2QH, England

Associated University Presses
2133 Royal Windsor Drive
Unit 1
Mississauga, Ontario
Canada L5J 1K5

Library of Congress Cataloging in Publication Data

Wilson, Jonathan, 1950–
  On Bellow's planet.

  Bibliography: p.
  Includes index.
  1. Bellow, Saul—Criticism and interpretation.
I. Title.
PS3503.E4488Z93   1985   813'.52   84-48449
ISBN 0-8386-3202-5

Printed in the United States of America

For Sharon Ann

Contents

Acknowledgments

This book began as a thesis for the Hebrew University of Jerusalem, although some of the groundwork was done at St. Catherine's College, Oxford. It has been with me through three countries and I have many debts to acknowledge along the way. In England there was Larzer Ziff, who guided my earliest reading in American literature, and Dudley Young of the University of Essex, whose thinking and writing about literature will always color my own. In Israel Baruch Hochman supervised my thesis with a kind heart and a strong hand. I could not have hoped for a better friend or a more thorough and scrupulous reader. The comments of Ken Dauber, Brian McHale and Eugene Goodheart contributed in the transformation of thesis to book. To Zali Gurevitch, Gill Grebler and Gabriel Levin I owe a debt of friendship that I hope to repay as I do to Lea Baider for the kind of support without which the book simply would not have been written. In America, I am grateful to Alan Lebowitz at Tufts, for offering me a fresh perspective on *Mr. Sammler's Planet,* and especially to Linda Bamber for some piquant editorial suggestions in the final stages. Martin Green of Fairleigh Dickinson University has helped in many ways, not the least being his belief that my reading of Bellow should see the light of day. Katharine Turok of Associated University Presses has been a most patient and considerate editor.

Finally, I am deeply grateful to my wife Sharon Kaitz, not only for her enduring support and willingness to talk Bellow but also for her wonderful paintings, a source of deep inspiration and pleasure whenever I lifted my head from a book.

Chapter 1 is an expanded version of an essay, "Bellow's Dangling Dean," which appeared in *The Literary Review* (Fall 1982). I am grateful to the editors for permission to reprint.

Introduction

In his famous essay on Tolstoy's philosophy of history, "The Hedgehog and the Fox," Isaiah Berlin, enlarging on Archilochus's line "the fox knows many things, but the hedgehog knows one big thing" divides writers and thinkers according to a figurative interpretation of the formulation. On one side are those who

> relate everything to a single central vision, one system less or more coherent or articulate, in terms of which they understand, think and feel . . . and, on the other side . . . those who pursue many ends, often unrelated and even contradictory, connected, if at all, only in some *de facto* way. . . . The first kind of intellectual and artistic personality belongs to the hedgehogs, the second to the foxes; and without insisting on a rigid classification, we may, without too much fear of contradiction, say that, in this sense Dante belongs to the first category, Shakespeare to the second; Plato, Lucretius, Pascal, Hegel, Dostoevsky, Nietzsche, Ibsen, Proust are, in varying degrees, hedgehogs; Herodotus, Aristotle, Montaigne, Erasmus, Molière, Goethe, Pushkin, Balzac, Joyce are foxes.[1]

Despite the foxy appearance of Saul Bellow's novels, in which an enormously wide range of seemingly disparate issues are discussed, his fiction is, I would suggest, the work of a "hedgehog." For, like Berlin's novelist/hedgehogs, Dostoevski and Proust, Bellow's novels articulate a system, a single vision of the world.

What is the "one big thing" that Bellow knows? Bellow sees the world much as Freud was beginning to see it when he outlined his bleak vision of the human predicament in *Civilization and Its Discontents.* The "big thing" that Freud knew in that book and that Bellow recapitulates in a fascinating way in his novels, is that the civilized world is a place where human beings are painfully and inevitably caught between their values on the one hand and their desires on the other. In Bellow's fictional world,

13

as in Freud's real one, the rewards of civilization—law, order, cleanliness, "civilized" behavior—are won at the expense of great individual frustration. Indeed, at some times it almost seems as if the psychology of Bellow's heroes has derived directly from Freud's assertion that civilized man has sacrificed much that would make him happy—including the acting out of his sexual and aggressive impulses—for the sake of security and protection. For, despite Bellow's sideswipes at Freud (most forcefully combined in his play *The Last Analysis*) our assessment and understanding of Bellow's central characters seems enhanced when we approach them as "living" examples of Freud's theories. Bellow's heroes, for the most part, live fairly comfortable, fairly "normal" lives: they are neither destitute, nor suffering excessively from disease, nor intolerably lonely, nor even "heartbroken." Nevertheless, they uniformly display a frustration and anger that, without recourse to notions of human suffering as the human condition, is almost ineffable.

The deep conflicts that Freud envisages between civilization and its discontents, order and disorder, cleanliness and dirt, are also central antitheses in Bellow's fiction. For example, reflection on Augie March's desire to settle down in the countryside and his simultaneous attraction to criminality will lead us to reflect on both his (and his society's) struggle with the relation of order to disorder, limitation to freedom. Similarly, when we discover Eugene Henderson "polluting" his neighborhood by establishing a pig farm on his rural estate and yet expressing a simultaneous desire to enter medical school, we are led to reflect on his ambivalent relationship to the ordered, civilized world. A large part of the experience of a Bellow hero will always be designed to illuminate or reflect his deeper conflict.

In this respect Bellow is (again) akin to Dostoevski, revealing his vision of the world through a world that he creates to support that vision. Dostoevski's fictional world is full of perverts, lunatics, drunks, prostitutes, and murderers, who are there, primarily, not because Saint Petersburg was overpopulated with such people, but because the terms of Dostoevski's governing dialectic demand that such characters exist to test it out. It is the same with Bellow. Bellow will not, or cannot image a wise man who is not also an eccentric, or a petty criminal, just as Dostoevski cannot, or will not, imagine a whore who does not have a golden heart or a murderer who is irredeemable.

The similarities (and they are deep ones) that exist between

Freud, Dostoevski and Bellow are, however, offset by significant differences in the attitudes that each adopts toward his own visions of the world. For, while Bellow's vision is bleak, it is neither tragic nor terrifying. This, I believe, is because the profound "thing" that Bellow knows is not always something that he wants to know. Unlike Freud, Bellow seems able to detach himself from his own insights into human nature—or at least to allow his characters to do so. As a result (and this is where Bellow parts company with Dostoevski) the terms of Bellow's governing dialectic, especially in his most recent novels, are often ghostly, unreal.

For Dostoevski the dialectical polarities that he established between, let us say, crime and punishment are vital forces, of the greatest importance to his heroes and palpably substantial to the author himself. By contrast, in Bellow's fiction from *Herzog* onward, the implied vision of the world—that it is difficult to inhabit and impossible to escape—is no longer central to the hero. Herzog (like Sammler, Citrine, and Corde) wryly contemplates his existence in the world as something "other" and is even able to regard his own divided personality from an ironic distance. What delights in Bellow's novels—his wit, irony, and comic detachment from the struggles of the quotidian—does so because it hurts not.

Paradoxically, then, Bellow's novels "progress" via the antitheses of what is really a "static dialectic": oppositions between order and chaos or limitation and freedom, upon whose resolution nothing hangs. As a result, the reader tends to be drawn to, or distracted by, the intellectual dance that hovers over and around the "static dialectic"—a dance that appears to give the novel fictional and ideological breadth and that leads us, mistakenly, to take Bellow for a "fox."[2] Interestingly, in his *Paris Review* interview (1965), Bellow took issue with Joyce, a writer whom he respects but with whom he has profound differences of opinion over the art of fiction. *Ulysses,* he says, is "the modern masterpiece of confusion." He goes on:

> There the mind is unable to resist experience. Experience in all its diversity, its pleasure and horror, passes through Bloom's head like an ocean through a sponge. The sponge can't resist; it has to accept what the waters bring. It also notices every micro-organism that passes through it. . . . Sometimes it looks as if the power of the mind has been nullified by the volume of experiences.[3]

Unlike Joyce, Bellow wishes to exert a greater control over the experience that passes through his heroes' heads. He does so because the recording of experience interests Bellow much less than its interpretation. Bellow's heroes, on the surface quite different beings, are all (with two exceptions) drawn from Bellow's imaginative conception of a single individual with a heightened consciousness, a man who is always confronted with a hostile world (not a protean world such as Joyce's) and who is never able to reconcile the contradictions inherent in his relation to that world. The experiences of a Bellow hero, which also display large surface differences, are actually all designed to relate back to a single set of governing ideas. As a result, Bellow's novels appear to move out into a fictional mimesis of a pluralistic world—but the appearance is misleading.

A critical "revision" of Bellow's novels, such as I must now declare this book to be, cannot really begin to go to work until it has confronted the critically popular notion that Bellow is, above all else, a "life-affirming" novelist. For, if what I have been suggesting is true, the irresolvably "static dialectic" of Bellow's novels would appear to fundamentally contradict the sense of open-ended human possibility that so many critics have discovered in Bellow's fiction. The assertion that Bellow is a "life-affirming novelist," I believe, does an injustice to Bellow both as a novelist and as a thinker. While it may sound perverse of me to take issue with critics for finding a writer "life-affirming," I do so because I believe it is a misreading that has obfuscated Bellow's fictive complexity and misrepresented his true relevance as a contemporary American writer. It must be acknowledged, however, that Bellow himself has played some part in misdirecting critical interpretations of his novels' themes and preoccupations.

The majority of Bellow's critics (and as Bellow keeps reminding us, we are now legion) find him to be a lone voice on the apocalyptic battlefields, still sounding the virtues of humanism, upholding the values of community, and beating back the emissaries of despair.[4] As I see it there are three major grounds on which this view has largely been based. The first is connected to Bellow's form,[5] the second to the supposed "affirmation" of his heroes,[6] and the last to what Bellow himself has said about his work and the work of others in his interviews, speeches, and discursive prose.[7]

Bellow's novels, for the most part, work within the confines of realistic fiction. Set against the interrupted massed structures of Pynchon or Barth, where the reader's natural search for a narrative hold is deliberately frustrated, Bellow's novels seem positively to invite the label "traditional." The postmodern form has long been seen as a schizophrenic response to a schizophrenic universe, a subjective vision in a world disintegrated into myriad "subjective visions." By contrast, the form of the traditional realistic novel has come to symbolize an ordered and governable world. Thus Bellow's realism is seen to constitute a mimesis of an ordered world and his narratives to imitate the order and "truth" that his novels so plangently affirm. Bellow's stories invite us to follow them, to see characters and to do all those things necessary for the imagination to be able to create a person called Augie March or Eugene Henderson.

Thus the very act of writing a novel in the realistic mode, in itself comes to seem an affirmative act implying an accurate mimesis of an ordered world. When, simultaneously, the novels' content is believed to be championing order and harmony, the effect is doubled. The contemporary realistic writer whose vision is brutal or "split" has the disadvantage of seeming to work against his chosen form.

Bellow's heroes have also been continuously imaged as affirmers. To a man they emphasize hope in the face of universal despair and attack the philosophers of doom and exponents of the "wasteland" mentality. Uniformly, they champion the extraordinary in the ordinary, the value of duty, the "aristocracy" of democratic man, the individuality of the mass man, and the indisputable meaning at the base of life. Each hero has his own moments of strong affirmation. "[C]haos doesn't run the whole show," Henderson says. "[T]his is not a sick and hasty ride, helpless, through a dream into oblivion. No, sir!" (*Henderson the Rain King*, p. 175). "We have our assignments," says Artur Sammler, "feelings, outgoingness, expressiveness, kindness, heart—all these fine human things which by a peculiar turn of opinion strike people now as shady activities" (*Mr. Sammler's Planet*, p. 303). Must "realism . . . be brutal?" (*Herzog*, p. 218) asks Herzog who cannot accept the "foolish dreariness" of "the commonplaces of the Wasteland outlook, the cheap mental stimulants of Alienation, the cant and rant of pipsqueaks about Inauthenticity and Forlorness" (*Herzog*, p. 75). For Augie March his "axial lines" of "Truth, love, peace, bounty, usefulness, harmony" are available to "any man at any time"

(*The Adventures of Augie March,* p. 454). Each in his turn, from
Joseph in *Dangling Man* to Albert Corde in *The Dean's December,*
finds space to uphold a set of positive values, to unfashionably
spit in the face of the doom-watchers.

What Bellow's heroes have to say on the subject finds en-
dorsement in the interviews, speeches, and discursive prose of
their creator. "There may be some truths which are, after all,
our friends in the universe,"[8] said Bellow in his 1965 *Paris Review* interview, a sentiment echoed in his Nobel Prize speech
(1976).[9] Attacks on existentialism abound in Bellow's writing,
where like his heroes, he has little or no time for what he terms
"complaint, stoicism . . . and nihilistic rage."[8]

> Writers like Sartre, Ionesco, and Beckett or like our own
> William Burroughs and Allen Ginsberg are only a few of the
> active campaigners on the shrinking front against the self.
> One would like to ask these contemporaries "After
> nakedness, what?" "After absurdity, what?"[9]

By contrast Bellow sees his own novels as opposing one of the
"dominant ideas of the century" exemplified in the work of
"Joyce, Celine and Mann, . . . that humankind has reached a
terminal point." The questions he sees himself as asking are
more vibrantly connected to affirmation and contingency:
"How can one resist the controls of this vast society *without*
turning into a nihilist, avoiding the absurdity of empty rebellion?" and "Are there other, more good-natured forms of resist-
ance and free choice?" By his own definition he has "involun-
tarily favored the more comforting and melioristic side of the
question."[10]

Critical responses to the novels, reinforced by the extramural
utterances of the writer himself, have thus combined to produce an image of Bellow as a gladiator fighting for meaning
and value for the "self." It is a "reading" of Bellow that I believe
to represent an error of some magnitude. Bellow's fiction, I
would suggest, projects a vision of the world as an essentially
hostile place populated, for the most part, by hypocrites, ego-
tists, grotesque swindlers, absolutists, and hardhearted "real-
ists." Where "good" does exist in Bellow's novels, as in the presentation of a "good" man like Elya Gruner *(Mr. Sammler's
Planet)* or Lucas Asphalter *(Herzog),* it is always called into question, undercut, and undermined, by making its appearance in a

grotesque form. Bellow's "best men" are always extremely eccentric or peripherally criminal.

Submerged in this harsh, unaccommodating world, Bellow's heroes persistently try to imagine a better one. While they are being persecuted, cheated, betrayed, or humiliated by their fellowmen, Bellow's heroes yet protest that, against all the evidence, the world must be at least half governed by a set of values that are positive and rewarding. Denying any objective validity to their own negative experience of the world, the heroes imagine a world of truth, order, harmony, and love to which they aspire, and to which they are sentimentally attached, but in which they never arrive.

It is partly Bellow's insistence on the centrality of these beneficent values as governing that has led critics to read him as so singularly life-affirming. As Lionel Trilling pointed out in *Sincerity and Authenticity,* the idea (in literature) that the "norm of life" should be one of "order, peace, honor and beauty" is an idea that we associate with Shakespeare and not with our apocalyptic twentieth-century novelists. According to Trilling, Bellow is almost unique in his positive assertions, so that as readers we are so shocked by his position that "we respond [to the novels] with discomfort and embarrassment."[11]

If the readers do respond with discomfort, I would like to suggest another possible reason for their doing so: their reaction to the indecisive "dangling" of Bellow's heroes, a dangling that drives them into uncomfortable dilemmas. And this dangling would seem to be, for heroes and Bellow both, congenital.

Bellow's heroes have always been the linchpins of his novels, and all of them share similar sets of problems and characteristics. Caught between their need for order in their lives and their propensity to create chaos, their yearning for freedom and their fear of anarchy, their desire for stillness and their fear of paralysis, Bellow's heroes persistently attack the objects of their own desire and behaviorally contradict their most cherished ideas. The list stretches all the way from Joseph in *Dangling Man* who, desiring "freedom," enlists in the army, through Charlie Citrine, the hero of *Humboldt's Gift,* who, flirting with ways of transcending the world altogether, involves himself in a complex set of criminal and erotic confusions, to Bellow's most recent hero, Albert Corde, a character whose life seems almost dedicated to ensuring that he will not be able to take the things he wants. In Bellow's canon, whoever searches for peace of

mind, like Moses Herzog, will of necessity attach himself to
someone who is guaranteed to bring chaos into his life; whoever yearns for stillness, like Augie March, is inevitably drawn
to spend his time in ceaseless travel.

The effect of such "dangling" is to contribute to the sense of
"not thereness" that emanates from all Bellow's heroes and that
critics have unanimously identified but rarely attempted to explain. This critical failure can, again, in part be attributed to a
general unwillingness to confront the contradictions inherent
in identifying Bellow as a "life-affirming" novelist. A hero who
is "not there"—either because he dissolves himself in his inner
contradictions or because his creator chooses to give him a
mind but not a body—is hardly an exemplary instance of life
affirmation.

"When we think of Saul Bellow what we think of is a certain
tone of voice,"[12] Gabriel Josipovici has aptly noted, and for most
critics, the answer to the "disembodiment" problem has been to
interpret a character's realization as if he existed almost solely
in the realm of ideas. Herzog, for example, who for Tony Tanner is "more of a presence than a person" and who for Irving
Howe is "not, in the traditional sense, a novelistic character at
all,"[13] is often responded to as if he were no more than the sum
of his ideas: an empty vessel, a crucible of ideological ex-
perimentation, but not a "personality" in the way that a familiar
hero of a great nineteenth-century novel might be. Viewed in
this light, one of the paradoxes of a Bellow novel reveals itself:
where central characters seek to castigate the proponents of
fixed ideas and ridicule the systematic conclusiveness of those
ideas, they nevertheless remain dependent upon them for a
sense of their own being.

The ground of the paradox, however, is not Bellow's interest
in ideas, or his heroes', but rather something radical in his
characters' makeup, something that, in one way or another,
unifies them. To a man, Bellow's heroes struggle to keep their
aggressive impulses (and to a lesser extent their sexual impulses) in check. Imaging themselves or imaged by a narrator
as wild spirits who curtail their behavior for the sake of a
civilized ethos, Bellow's heroes submit to a behavioral pattern
that requires that they deny their deepest feelings.

Bellow's heroes are generally frustrated and are always
searching for a new life. However, it is not always altogether
clear what they are frustrated with or angry about. The answer

seems to lie in their more or less conscious apprehension (dependent upon the heroes' intelligence and insight) that in their present adult lives they cannot have things as they would like them to be.

Unable either to have their own way or the world that they desire, some of Bellow's heroes (Leventhal, Wilhelm) harbor a childish petulance that for the most part manifests itself in an expression of personal anguish and anger. One of the defining characteristics of Bellow's heroes is their barely repressed violence. Four of Bellow's heroes—Leventhal, Augie, Wilhelm, and Herzog—own up to having murder in their hearts, and the plots of the novels are punctuated with outbursts of violent behavior. Joseph assaults his landlord and his niece; Leventhal shoves Allbee around; Augie sets off to kill his girlfriend's lover; Wilhelm throttles himself when indicating what we presume he would really like to be doing to his wife; Henderson has a voice that can (and does) kill; and Herzog gets hold of a gun with the intention of shooting his ex-wife Madeleine and her lover Gersbach. In every case, however, the hero seems conscious of the fact that violence and murder are extremely "uncivilized," and thus anathema to him. It is this self-awareness—a sense of his instincts as base and therefore necessitating repression—that seems to contribute so much to the Bellow hero's sense of pain and frustration.

Anxious about the necessity of repressing their aggression, Bellow's heroes fuel their frustration by agonizing over the fact that they cannot get the amount of love that they want. A salient characteristic of the Bellow hero is his overwhelming need to be loved by a brother, parent, or woman who does not seem overly interested in loving him. Augie's relationship with his brother Simon *(The Adventures of Augie March);* Charlie's with his brother Julius *(Humboldt's Gift);* Tommy Wilhelm's with his father, Dr. Adler *(Seize the Day);* and Herzog's with his ex-wife Madeleine all attest to the heroes' "childish" insistence that those he loves love him back with an equal, if not greater, intensity.

Unable to express his anger and unable to secure the amount of love that he wants, the Bellow hero is, almost perversely, convinced that violence is a sin and love imprisoning. Always presented as child/men, Bellow's heroes straddle the worlds of innocence and experience. They are both Blake's clod and his pebble.

The recurring pattern of a Bellow novel is one in which the hero, in a state of deep personal crisis, tries to take stock of his situation. Invariably he appears to be caught in a horrific personal limbo and the inhabitant of a predominantly hostile society. Burdened by his everyday life, usually in financial difficulty, and plagued by a demanding ex-wife, the Bellow hero apparently has nowhere to turn. However, practically all Bellow's heroes sustain themselves by falling back on their intellects and imaginations. Like Moses Herzog, who claims that he "inflames himself with his own drama" (*Herzog,* p. 208), Bellow's solipsistic characters turn inward for their mental sustenance. Unlike, say, Stendhal's "egoists" who, despite their protean selves, persistently redefine themselves through action, Bellow's heroes compensate for their lack of identity by distracting themselves with the complex figurations of their own minds.

What we apprehend in Bellow's fiction is not, however, a protagonist who is merely the sum of his ideas but one whose "mind"—a mixture of memory, fantasy, creative imagination, and ideas—becomes the substance of the novel. It is the mind of a highly unique individual. To a man central characters in Bellow claim not to know "who they are." As such they easily become receptacles for ideas, for they are constantly testing out versions of reality or of identity in an apparent attempt to solve their own "identity" and "reality" problems.

The void at the hero's center is repeatedly filled and emptied as the novels progress, ideas are swallowed and regurgitated. Naturally, the more of a thinker the hero is, the more ideas he will have, *but* the passage of ideas in and out of a hero's consciousness always leaves him fundamentally unchanged. Normally, in the process of the novels, Bellow's heroes come through some kind of personal crisis, but there is rarely any convincing hint that they have broken a pattern. Whatever Bellow's heroes are is not defined by what they think of Rousseau or Tolstoy or the U.S. presidency.

Solitary figures, and, for the most part, sophisticated thinkers, Bellow's heroes, perhaps surprisingly, are not artists or writers. They do not belong to a group that we would conventionally associate with a strong sense of alienation or cultural frustration. However, they suffer in much the same way as the artist-heroes of so many twentieth-century novels. Highly energetic personalities, who often seem to embody a creative potential, they uniformly lack an artistic vocation. The paralysis of Bellow's early heroes seems (especially in the cases of Joseph and Augie) somehow to be tied to their inability to play out the role that in the work of another novelist we might have expected to find them in. Alienated, and powerless, Bellow's heroes are apparently as individual as any Romantic artist. But the role of "artist" seems to be as threatening to the Bellow hero as all of the other roles—doctor/criminal/businessman/ academic/dean that he finds it so hard to let himself play.

Bellow's "late" heroes—Herzog, Sammler, Citrine, and Corde—are more content than their predecessors to occupy the traditional position of the artist in American society. Unlike Joyce's Stephen Dedalus or Proust's Marcel, however, these heroes have no redeeming aesthetic vision but, outcast and peripheral, they find compensation in the complex workings of their own minds. Moreover, and perhaps more significantly, they are more consciously aware than any of Bellow's other heroes of the way in which their personal crises serve to enlighten them. The "insight" of those Bellow heroes who have it is always partly derived from the state of excitement that their personal crises throw them into. The energy of Bellow's heroes can almost be defined as the energy of paralysis. Artur Sammler says that he is "obliged to events for a intensification of vision" (*Mr. Sammler's Planet,* p. 43), and this is true of all Bellow's heroes whether or not they welcome such an increase in their perceptive powers. Unable to find a place for themselves (and anyway unwilling to do so), unable to resolve their crises, and unable to have the world as they would like it to be, Bellow's heroes are all partly sustained (consciously or unconsciously) by the almost masochistic pleasure that their "paralysis" gives them.

For the Bellow hero, crises are stimulating: not only do they allow him to experience "fits of vividness" and "demonic excitement" (*The Dean's December,* p. 151), but also the "paralysis" that they induce permits him to temporarily forgo all kinds of adult responsibilities.

Invariably, at some point in a Bellow novel, we will discover the hero to be locked into a paralyzing relationship with a dominating wife, lover, companion, or relative. Often, we are given to understand that the hero has sought out this relationship against his own better interests. However, while the hero tends to remain ambivalent as to the pros and cons of his subsequent passivity, he clearly always derives some pleasure from

being directed, looked after, or told what to do. The Bellow
hero is most himself when, like Augie March, he is giving himself up "to another guy's scheme" (*The Adventures of Augie
March,* p. 456). Most often he gives himself up to the schemes of
some kind of father figure: elder brothers like Simon (*The Adventures of Augie March*), Will (*Herzog*), or Julius (*Humboldt's
Gift*); cranks like Dahfu (*Henderson the Rain King*) or Tamkin
(*Seize the Day*); or criminals like Joe Gorman (*The Adventures of
Augie March*) and Rinaldo Cantabile (*Humboldt's Gift*). Interestingly, one of the attractions of these father figures seems to be
the release that they often offer from the domination of a
mother figure.

Problematic women in Bellow's canon may be divided into
two types: the "hags" who afflict Bellow's younger heroes—
Joseph's mother-in-law in *Dangling Man,* the old Italian grand-
mother in *The Victim,* or Grandma Lausch (*The Adventures of
Augie March*); and the "bitches" who make life miserable for the
more mature personalities—Thea Fenchel (*The Adventures of
Augie March*), Margaret (*Seize the Day*), Frances (*Henderson the
Rain King*), Madeleine (*Herzog*), and Denise (*Humboldt's Gift*). Of
this latter group, Thea Fenchel is notably less bitchy than her
successors, presumably because she never manages to ensnare
the hero of the novel in which she appears into an imprisoning
marriage.

For the "mature" Bellow hero, escape from demanding and
controlling women often takes the form of a lengthy and complex affair with another woman. However, all the mistresses—
Stella (*The Adventures of Augie March*), Olive (*Seize the Day*), Lily
(*Henderson the Rain King*), Ramona (*Herzog*), and Renata (*Humboldt's Gift*)—are potential wives and as such contain within
them the potential to be as destructive, manipulative, and ultimately as castrating as their rivals—the present wives.[14] In the
company of men the Bellow hero is safer. In the company of
"father figures" the hero will be controlled but fewer demands
will be made upon him. The pressure to become an adult is
reduced and consequently the fact that the hero is "paralyzed"
becomes, for him, both painful and pleasurable.

Some critics have found in the predicament of Bellow's
heroes a condition that is representatively American. For Malcolm Bradbury, Herzog's inability to decide whether he is
"formed" or "forming," "necessarily small," or able to achieve a
"fullness of self" can be described this way.[15] It is the particular
nature of Bellow's fictional concern with "the relative status of

historical and environmental determinism" and its effect on "concepts of the individual self" that, for Bradbury, define and reveal Bellow's novelistic "roots": Bradbury finds *Herzog,* for example, a novel "deeply located in its society, the society of urban America, and this society is much more deeply located in its founding history and ideology."[16]

For Tony Tanner, Bellow's heroes are exemplary modern American protagonists in that they appear to be caught uncomfortably between a desire for identity and a desire for freedom from the societal patterning that would provide it. Bellow's heroes, caught between "fixity and flow" plump for what Tanner neatly calls "flexibility"; in doing so they enact a fundamental American rhythm that embodies the anxious and classic American fear that "that which *de*fines you at the same time *con*fines you."[17]

The question that begs itself, it seems to me, is the extent to which Bellow's idiosyncratic heroes can be viewed as representative Americans. It is one of the oddities of Bellow's modes of characterization that he seems to want the reader to identify his hero both as a "mid-American" (an "out and out Chicagoan") and as a character well outside the mainstream. If Bellow's heroes are representative Americans, I would suggest that they come closest to being so in the state of mind that they typify. It is perhaps a measure of middle-class American life that a "paralyzed" hero who is afraid of the society he inhabits and terrified of alternative societies should become so popular. If America is reflected in Bellow, it is the America of those citizens (liberals?) who, wanting to believe that reality does not have to be brutal, perpetually discover it to be unbearably so; and who are obsessed with visions that they are unable to realize and with a reality that they are unable to accept.

Bellow's novels may begin as attempts to say something grand about America, or to isolate specifically American problems, but if they end up by doing so it is only, as it were, by default. For Bellow's fiction increasingly reveals itself as concentrating more significantly on the individual quirks and thought processes of a single mind. If, with *The Adventures of Augie March* Bellow had attempted to write the Great American Novel, he soon abandoned the task and began working toward the more strictly limited *Henderson the Rain King* and *Herzog*— works that are never discussed as *The* Great American novel but rather as great American novels.

Bellow's novels, I would suggest, finally reveal far more to us about their author than they do about the country in which he lives. The work of a solipsistic writer whose novels gradually become increasingly autobiographical, Bellow's fiction presents a series of brilliant characterizations—particular studies of a single American life. What primarily interests Bellow, undoubtedly, as he grows older, is himself. Our response to his novels will finally be governed by the extent to which we share his fascination. We must be prepared to follow his heroes in the world, but, perhaps, not to see the world in his heroes.

Part One

Seasons in the Interior

1 —————

The Dean's December

To begin with a reading of *The Dean's December*, which I believe to be the least successful of Bellow's nine novels, may seem an odd place to commence a full-length study of his work. However, I have two reasons for doing so: the first is connected to the novel itself, the second to the vantage point that it gives us on the rest of Bellow's fiction.

The overriding bleakness of *The Dean's December*—and it is surely the bleakest novel in the canon—derives not so much from its despairing vision of the decline of the West, set against the demise of Eastern Europe, but rather from the strong feeling it communicates that its author has lost interest or has a diminished interest in creating fiction. For, while it is studded with the passages of descriptive brilliance that are Bellow's hallmark and while it is enlivened with flashes of wit and insight, *The Dean's December* remains a skeletal work. The almost characterless insubstantiality of its protagonist Albert Corde coupled with the general thinness of the world that he inhabits and the near invisibility of the minor characters who surround him report a detachment on Bellow's part that is readily transferred to the reader. However, "stripped bare" in this way, *The Dean's December* also lays bare the dialectical machinery of Bellow's fiction and points up both his strengths and weakness as a novelist.

In addition to providing a kind of blueprint of Bellow's method, *The Dean's December* enables us to look back on Bellow's earlier fiction with fresh insight. For it now seems to me that Bellow has been moving toward the strained fictionality of *The Dean's December* for some time and that the elements in his fiction that are presently causing it to disintegrate are the same elements that have all along been providing the creative dynamic of his novels. My intention is not to deny Bellow's brilliance as a novelist, to call into question the rich expressiveness of *The Adventures of Augie March,* the comic genius of *Henderson the Rain King,* or the intellectual triumph of *Herzog,* but rather to understand what it is in Bellow's work that lends it the strange air of fiction constantly carrying the seeds of its own destruction. An analysis of *The Dean's December* grants us some insights into that process, and they are insights that help to illuminate all the novels that precede it.

The novel begins effectively enough with Bellow's powerful evocation of Bucharest in winter. The Rumanian capital, with its gray Communist residential blocks and brown December twilights, is called up with all the grace of accuracy that in earlier novels Bellow has reserved for Chicago and New York. At the heart of this gloomy cityscape, sequestered in a minimally furnished room, sipping plum brandy to keep away the December chills, we find Bellow's eponymous hero, Dean Albert Corde.

A "journalist, highbrow professor, dean and intellectual" (p. 88), Corde has come from Chicago with his Rumanian-born wife in order to pay what is probably to be a last visit to her dying mother. Back in Chicago, Corde has left behind a double crisis that is for him both personal and public. A student in the college where he is dean has been murdered; a black whore and her pimp have been arrested and accused. Implicated in their capture, by his role in having ensured that a reward was posted, Corde has found himself the target of angry student radicals. He is accused of being a racist and his chief accuser is none other than his own nephew. To make matters worse, the defending counsel in the trial is Corde's first cousin, Max Detillion, a man determined, for reasons of long-standing personal animosity, to drag Corde's name through the mud.

The second of Corde's crises is more of his own devising. He has written a series of articles on Chicago that have been published in *Harper*'s magazine. Corde's topics—the anarchy of the streets, the corruption of governors and government, the horror of prison conditions, ghetto slums, and "the slums of the innermost being" (p. 201)—have managed to offend almost everybody. Most significantly, they have caused embarrassment to Corde's college and, at the moment of his departure for Bucharest, Corde is seriously out of favor with his provost, Alec Witt.

As in *Humboldt's Gift,* the novel that immediately precedes *The Dean's December,* it seems for the first fifty pages or so as if

Bellow is going to introduce and develop a wide range of characters and themes. However, just as in the earlier novel, where neither the narrator Charlie Citrine nor Bellow himself was able to sustain his interest in portraying the "poet-king" (*Humboldt's Gift*, p. 25), Von Humboldt Fleisher and his attendant lords Ambition and Frustration, so too in *The Dean's December*, Corde's (and Bellow's) interest in the characters who surround him—the dying Valeria, his wife Minna, the host of persecutors in Chicago—quickly wanes.

Having announced that he will bear witness to "Great Valeria's end" (p. 7) and having introduced a character called Petrescu who "played a leading part in the emotional composition whose theme was Valeria's last days," Corde is quick to abandon both subjects in favor of a closer look at his own emotional composition. As the reader is drawn in to Corde's self-absorbed internal world, the external world that he inhabits begins to lose its distinction. Bucharest and Chicago fade into the background and minor characters lean back into their own invisibility. Before we have had time to catch our breath, Albert Corde's directing consciousness and not "Great Valeria's end" has ineluctably become the true subject of the novel.

The inward lurch that *The Dean's December* takes hardly comes as a surprise. *Herzog, Mr. Sammler's Planet,* and *Humboldt's Gift* are all novels that have largely taken place within the heads of their protagonists. What is surprising is Bellow's subsequent failure to animate Corde's personality. Since *Herzog,* the pressure on Bellow's central figures to carry the ideational weight and to convey the moral depth of the novels in which they appear has greatly increased. As a consequence, the "risk" that Bellow now takes in his novels is a large one. For, should the quality of his hero's consciousness fail to inspire the reader or should the hero's "higher thoughts" prove less than fascinating, the novel is likely to fail.

On the face of it, Albert Corde seems very much the familiar Bellow hero, caught between a need for order in his life and a propensity to create chaos. Holding a post that connotes stability and authority, Corde despises the university institution that has both offered and preserved for him the orderly life that he has desired. Believing, apparently, in maintaining the status quo, Corde impulsively puts his job in jeopardy by writing the "embarrassing" Chicago articles. When, a little less than halfway through the novel, Corde comes to ask himself the familiar

Bellovian question, "What *did* [he] represent? Who was this person? . . . ?" (p. 131), the reader knows enough about him to be able to reply quite confidently: You are a close relation of the heroes who came before you. You are a character unable to affirm or deny either yourself or the world that you inhabit. You are unsure if you yourself are wise or foolish—"an earnest, brooding, heart-struck, time-ravaged person (or boob). . . ." (p. 122); adult or child—"He wondered what it might mean about him as a 'serious adult' that the flowers should claim so much of his attention" (p. 79). However, the general drift of the narrative in which you appear is aimed at convincing us that your naiveté is really insight and your childishness profundity. You feel oppressed by the limitations that your society places on your life, but you are just as troubled by your notion of what constitutes freedom, because in your mind it often amounts to the same thing as "chaos." You are, for want of a better expression, and as your name implies, Mr. Corde, a "dangling man."

In *The Dean's December*, however, despite these similarities that link him to his predecessors, Albert Corde signally fails to arouse the reader's interest. A deep regression has occurred, for, like the characters who surround him, Corde has become something of a cipher. Why should this be when so much of what Corde thinks seems to repeat, in wit, intensity, and insight, the entertaining (if troublesome) thoughts of Bellow's other heroes?

The compelling reason for Bellow's inability to transform Albert Corde into an interesting character is, I believe, connected to the convergence (or, in this case, to the *lack* of convergence) of autobiography and fiction in Bellow's novels. Since the publication of *Herzog*, Bellow has more or less chosen to fictionally reconstitute himself in the person of his novels' protagonists. What *The Dean's December* unwittingly reveals is just how vital the proximity of author to hero has been to the continuing success of Bellow's late fiction.

In *The Dean's December*, Albert Corde is given a consciousness that approximates so closely that of Moses Herzog and Charlie Citrine that it is a shock to find him dressed not in the clothes of a Jewish academic type but rather in those of a *WASP.* If it sounds like prejudice to suggest that Corde is less authentic as a hero because he is a WASP, then Bellow must bear the brunt of the blame. For, he has powerfully convinced us that a mind with the particular nuances of Corde's can only exist within the body of a certain type of hero. A hero with a personal history that corresponds to Bellow's own.

It is no secret that Herzog and Citrine are autobiographical figures.[1] Until the publication of *The Dean's December,* I had tended to believe that Bellow's self-consumption was detrimental to his fiction. However it now appears that Herzog and Citrine may well have drawn their fictive authenticity from the autobiographical elements in their makeup. It is paradoxical and ironic that when Bellow halfheartedly attempts to "imagine" a personal history for Albert Corde, the result is to render him inauthentic and even less "present" than his predecessors.

An eighth-generation American of Huguenot-Irish descent—"We were leftovers of the Louisiana Purchase, Napoleon sold us all to Thomas Jefferson so he could pay for his invasion of Russia" (pp. 177–78)—Corde's social identity seems only a cloak of disguise that Bellow has peremptorily draped over his shoulders in mock obeisance to the Art of Fiction. Bellow's other late heroes are disembodied, in that they exhibit an almost postmortem detachment to their own experience, but their "visiting consciousness" (*Mr. Sammler's Planet,* p. 73) nevertheless appear to inhabit the right shells. Because his consciousness has been dislocated, Albert Corde fails to achieve the "existence" that, say, Herzog and Citrine do. As a result something very odd occurs. Instead of responding to Corde from the information that we are given in the novel, the reader is drawn to flesh out his personality from what he knows of Bellow's other heroes. Bizarre as this may sound, it often seems as if Bellow is actually inviting us to perform such an imaginative act.

Apart from the brief sketch of Corde's background and a description of his father as a "Pullman-car type" (p. 16), we learn very little of Corde's personal history. Our understanding of him, I would suggest, is constantly augmented by and dependent upon our prior understanding of the motivating forces that govern the behavior of the protagonists of the earlier novels. For example, Corde makes repeated reference to his infamous former "erotic instability" (pp. 9, 53, 198)—a behavioral propensity about which we are given no further information. Corde frets because he wishes his dying mother-in-law to rest assured that, since meeting her daughter, he is a changed man: a trustworthy and reliable husband. Yet, the credibility of

Corde's having had a swinger's past seems somehow to depend on our knowledge of the love lives of Moses Herzog, Charlie Citrine, and, presumptively, on knowledge of Bellow himself.

The Dean's December is one of the few Bellow novels in which the married hero does not have a mistress or several mistresses. It is also the first novel in which the hero is happily married.[2] Because we never know how or why Corde has won his reputation for "erotic instability" and because in so many other ways his consciousness corresponds to that of his predecessors, the reader is imaginatively drawn to fill in the background with Herzog's Sono Oguki and Ramona, Citrine's Doris Scheldt and Renata. Corde can be trusted as a husband because he has found what Herzog and Citrine were looking for: a marriage that does not imprison, a love that does not enchain.

The temptation to view Corde not in terms of himself but in those of some other hero is enhanced by our response to his relationship with a childhood friend Dewey Spangler. A "big-shot opinion-maker" (p. 67), a journalist with access to the highest echelons of political power, Spangler turns up in Bucharest to do a series of interviews with the local dictator. With the aid of his "formidable memory" (p. 112), Corde is able to undercut Spangler mercilessly by bringing to mind and mouth the journalist's scrofulous, "plucked chicken" (p. 239) adolescence. In their meetings, the two characters enact a familiar Bellovian drama. Corde feels both affection and loathing for his avuncular, patronizing friend. Trusting Spangler, he is eventually betrayed by him when some offhand remarks of Corde's about college professors find their way into Spangler's column. Like so many paternalistic figures in Bellow's canon (who, given Bellow's propensity to avoid direct confrontations between fathers and sons, are usually brothers or friends), Spangler is set up only to be knocked down. If Corde is, in Spangler's view, "a grown man allowing himself to regress" (p. 120) because he clings to a poetic vision and displays a loyalty to things of the spirit, the reader cannot help but get the impression that the real fool is Spangler.

As his name playfully suggests, Spangler is the true instance of the Decline of the West: the politics in which he traffics are merely a surface reality. However, and most importantly, the relationship between the two characters seems to distort the authentic sense of social history that Bellow is usually so careful to convey. Spangler is clearly Jewish, from a poor background,

and, like many of Bellow's Jewish protagonists, has been entranced as an adolescent with "Shakespeare . . . Rilke . . .
Nietzsche" (p. 118). Equally entranced, the gentile Corde became Spangler's best high school buddy.

As one of the reviewers of *The Dean's December* suggested, it is
not impossible that forty years ago, boys of Huguenot Irish
backgrounds hung out in the parks of Chicago with their Jewish friends, poring over Blake and Spinoza, yet "to merely assume this is to obscure a precious social phenomenon."[3] That
such literary enthusiasm informed the nature of Jewish American social life (and that of the Jewish social life of Bellow's other
novels) is, as the same critic points out, a feature of American
history; Bellow "does justice neither to the world nor to the
imagination by constructing social histories according to purely
personal agendas."

Albert Corde lacks both a convincing socio-historical reality
and a defining personal history. Bellow's failure to turn Corde
into an engaging protagonist seems to confirm what has been
apparent since *Herzog,* that Bellow cannot work up much interest in creating central figures who are "Other"—who do not
throw back mirror images of his own self. Moreover, what the
protrayal of Corde reveals is that the elements in Bellow's history that he now apparently finds least interesting—his childhood; his relationships with friends, lovers, and relatives—are
those that when "fictionalized" lend authenticity to his heroes.
For, while Corde expresses "political" and philosophical ideas
that are close to Bellow's and while he repeats a journey to
Bucharest that Bellow himself recently made, he does not assume Bellow's personal history.

Unfortunately, as far as the vitality of *The Dean's December* is
concerned, when the "personal history" is discarded, so too are
all those mesmerizing and edifying bitches and bullies who so
enliven the novels in which they appear. What we are left with
in *The Dean's December* is a series of dry intellectual messages:
Bellow's *Weltanschauung* without Bellow's world.

The level of generalization in Bellow's fiction has always been
high. However, it is extremely difficult to make generalizations
about America or, "the American personality" from Bellow's
novels. For his deep concern, as *The Dean's December* puts beyond argument, is with the world of a single individual: an
individual whose outer form alters but whose inner life changes
very little. Back in the fifties, Norman Mailer noted that "Bel-

low's one major weakness . . . is that he creates individuals and not the relations between them."[4] What Bellow does do, as if to compensate these individuals for their loneliness, is to spread his heroes' consciousnesses all over the novel.

Increasingly, in the novels published since *Henderson,* description of the social world has become for Bellow not a means of reporting America but rather of reproducing as accurately as possible the internal antagonisms of his hero. In all Bellow's novels the dominance of the central character is affected and attenuated by the symbolic representation of his inner conflict in the outer world. Minor characters and description of the environment embody parts of the hero's inner world and, as a result, the relation between the hero and his world is often symbolically reflexive. If the central character is torn between "order" and "disorder," there will be minor characters aligned on both sides of the fence. In *Mr. Sammler's Planet,* for example, two characters, Elya Gruner and a black pickpocket, initially represent opposite poles of honesty and crime, goodness and evil, and the hero, Artur Sammler, is (confusingly for him) drawn magnetically to both of them. Bellow's method is, of course, far from unique and in fact is recognizable as a pervasive tendency in literature (we might think of Hal flanked by Hotspur and Falstaff). But what is problematic is that his minor characters no longer manage to develop beyond their cipher-like symbolic presence.[5]

In *The Dean's December* this is more than ever so. Largely governed by his own contradictory needs to, on the one hand, lead a quiet life of marital bliss and, on the other, to involve himself in controversial and potentially dangerous issues and events, Corde finds himself involved with characters who seem to metaphorically extend his own problems. In Chicago Corde is answerable to a provost whose notions of college decorum he finds arbitrary and inhibiting, and he is also responsible to a student population, represented by his nephew Morton Zaehner, whose demands he finds foolishly anarchistic and potentially destructive. However, neither the provost nor Zaehner ever suggest that they are anything other than symbolic presences: they are Corde's own devils and they whisper in his ears as he sits uncomfortably between them.

On a larger scale, the setting of the novel is also divided between representatives of Order and Chaos. The time and action shift from East to West, from Bucharest to Chicago. In

Eastern Europe, Corde is witness to totalitarian cruelty, to arbitrary order at its most unnerving and ridiculous. His Rumanian-born wife is refused visiting rights to her dying mother. A colonel of the secret police sadistically teases the Cordes by offering them visiting rights if they agree to a change of hospital for the patient—the new hospital does not possess the machines to keep Valeria alive. Aside from his personal experiences, Corde, in a more general way, cannot help but note the fear, circumspection, and hint of betrayal implicit in practically every human transaction that is undertaken in Bucharest.

However, the nightmare of life under a dictatorship seems only slightly more terrifying than the bad dream of life in America. In Chicago Corde bears witness to the detritus of crime and hardship brought down upon the city by the inadequacy of its governors, the unmitigated violence of its criminals, and, perhaps most important of all, the spiritual vacuity of its law-abiding, conative citizens. Bellow has always been adept at transmitting the atmosphere of a city (most brilliantly in *The Adventures of Augie March*), but the cities in his most recent novels are ultimately maps of a single consciousness rather than representations of urban life. The city is at the service of an Idea: the "Idea" that the world is irrevocably split in the same way as its representative Bellovian inhabitant.

Gradually, it seems to me, in the second half of his career as a novelist, Bellow has been methodically dismantling the House of Fiction that he carefully constructed in the first half of his career. Where once, as we shall see, Bellow's pages were filled with inspirational minor characters like Grandma Lausch and William Einhorn in *The Adventures of Augie March*, Adler and Tamkin in *Seize the Day*, or King Dahfu in *Henderson the Rain King*, characters who maintained a distracting personality of their own, there now stalk more shadowy concoctions: Govinda Lal in *Mr. Sammler's Planet*, Humboldt himself in *Humboldt's Gift*, Minna, Petrescu, Zaehner, and Witt in *The Dean's December*. Where once the "not thereness" of the heroes was redeemed by the richness of the fictional landscapes that surrounded them— the detailed worlds of New York and Chicago in *The Victim* and *The Adventures of Augie March*, the perfectly captured ambience of the Upper West Side in *Seize the Day*—there now exist environments designed almost exclusively, it sometimes seems, to metaphorically extend the internal conflicts of the heroes.

At the close of *The Dean's December*, we find Corde, his

troubles largely behind him, inside the giant telescope at Mount
Palomar, ascending toward the stars with his astronomer wife.
Moving between heaven and earth, between the coldness of the
stars and that of the "death house" (p. 311), between an intimation of transcendence and one of mortality, Corde momentarily
feels that he would like to remain suspended, gazing into the
enveloping starlit semidarkness, rather than return to earth. It
is a moment of cold, dispassionate beauty that also perfectly
encapsulates the state of mind of Bellow's late heroes, and perhaps of Bellow's current attitude toward his fiction.

Corde aspires to transcend a world in which he can no longer
generate a sustaining interest. Yet the infinite stars are all too
ready to "draw him in": Halfway is best. What remains to interest Corde and Bellow are not crises on earth nor the "tensions
. . . in the living heavens" but the tensions in his head.

2

Dangling Man

Despite the almost four decades that separate *Dangling Man* from *The Dean's December,* the current bookends of Bellow's canon have much in common. Both novels are stark winters' tales dependent for their light on the vivid interior worlds of their respective protagonists. Like Albert Corde, Joseph, the hero of *Dangling Man,* is a sequestered individual, confined for most of his novel to a grubby Chicago rooming house. Beyond the closed windows of Joseph's apartment, chill winds, fog, and deep winter darkness contribute to an environment that is altogether as gloomy as Albert Corde's Bucharest. As in *The Dean's December,* however, the haunting exterior world is evoked only sporadically. Moreover, minor characters are as shadowy in *Dangling Man* as they are in the later novel.

On the surface, the similarities between the two novels may be attributed to the odd correspondence that the tentativeness of Bellow's early work has with his present "afictionality." However, a coupling of the two novels also reveals a more integral sameness.

For, Joseph is Bellow's prototypical "dangling man" and the novel in which he appears anticipates, in a smaller orbit, the concerns and preoccupations of Bellow's entire canon.

Dangling Man takes the form of a diary and, like all Bellow's novels, it centers on the consciousness of a single individual. Joseph (we never learn his last name) is a young, married man awaiting induction into the U.S. army. The year is 1942, so his is not a simple case of national service. The world in turmoil is, however, offstage in this novel and what preoccupies reader, author, and protagonist is Joseph's inner turmoil. Having given up his clerical job with the "Inter-American Travel Bureau" (p. 10) in anticipation of an early call-up, Joseph finds himself in limbo when bureaucratic complications surrounding his

Canadian (and thereby British) citizenship come between himself and the army. Seven months of waiting have gone by when we are first introduced to him through the pages of his diary, and another four months of entries are to occupy the reader until Joseph finally sidesteps the red tape by volunteering.

With more time on his hands than he knows what to do with, Joseph gives himself over to meditations on his own and the human condition. Late in the novel, he describes his fellow Chicagoans as spending "a long winter in the interior" (p. 169), and the same might be said of Joseph himself.

Between leaving his job and joining the army, Joseph labors under the burdens of a man caught between differing, and often contradictory, senses of himself and of the world. Marking time, his personality undergoes a radical transformation, and he draws sharp distinctions between his "old self" and his "new self." On the fundamental dichotomy of these two selves,. Joseph constructs a set of ideational opposites that are at once the substance of the novel and the dialectical underpinning of Bellow's thought.

Where Joseph's "old self" regards the world as fundamentally crude but beneficent if "controlled" in the right way, his "new self" views it as predominantly hostile and uncontrollable. Where the "old self" conceives of man as instinctually drawn towards goodness, the "new self" tends to regard man as a murderous creature who is obliged to repress his deepest instincts for the sake of civilization.

Joseph's "older self" (p. 26) is "not severe towards the world" (p. 29). Numbering himself among "visionaries" (p. 29), his vision is of a world neither

> wholly good or wholly malevolent. . . . Of those who believe in a wholly good world he says that they do not understand depravity. As for pessimists, the question he asks of them is, "Is that all they see, such people?" For him, the world is both and therefore it is neither. (P. 29)

But this older self does not bow to the status quo; "he" is a meliorist whose faith is placed in such notions as that of "common humanity" (p. 25) and moreover he is full of a sense of "wonder" strong enough to enable him to say without irony that

in a sense, everything is good because it exists. Or good or
not good, it exists, it is ineffable and for that reason marvellous. (Pp. 29–30)

The only black mark in the "older self's" copybook is the fact
that along with his communal yearnings he "suffers from a
feeling of strangeness, or not quite belonging to the world"
(p. 30). The combination of his philosophy and his feelings
metaphorically align this "older self" with Joseph's status in the
United States at the beginning of the war—he is a "friendly
alien" (p. 11). By contrast, we may characterize Joseph's newer
self as an "unfriendly alien." His world is unaccommodating, a
place where natural "generosity and good will" are of necessity
turned to "bitterness and spite" (p. 12). The "new" Joseph has
deployed a Hobbesian sense of life as "'nasty, brutish and
short'" (p. 40) and has resigned himself to the authority of
darkness.

Along with his new and depressing insights into the true
nature of the world, Joseph has also come to see himself in a
less than favorable light. Where once he had conceived of himself as a separate personality "keeping intact and free from
encumbrance a sense of his own being, its importance" (p. 27),
he now tends to regard himself as inconsequential. Where once
he believed that the individual was capable of exercising control
over his own fate, he now feels that "the world comes after you
[and] singles you out for this part or that" (p. 137).

Joseph, then, presents himself as a character who has shifted
ground, someone who first thought one thing but has been led
by a new set of experiences to think another. From the reader's
point of view, however, the transition that he claims to have
made from "optimistic" to "pessimistic" self is less than convincing. For, as the novel progresses, Joseph is revealed to us as a
divided personality, one who simultaneously entertains antithetical notions of the world and of the self. Bellow's interest, it
turns out, is not in Joseph's philosophical "development" but in
the rending of his personality as it is brought about by his
pervasive "dangling."

The questions that haunt Joseph—Is the world hospitable or
alien? Does humankind have a capacity for greatness or are we
merely the "feeble-minded children of angels?" (p. 137)—are
also questions that haunt Bellow. What *Dangling Man* and Bel-

low's other novels seem to insist upon is that a choice be made. Paradoxically, they also seem to insist that such a choice is impossible to make. Joseph himself outlines the problem in terms of the varying demands that our knowledge of death and our experience of life make upon us.

> Great pressure is brought to bear to make us undervalue ourselves. On the other hand, civilization teaches us that each is an inestimable prize. . . . Therefore we value and are ashamed to value ourselves. . . . (P. 119)

Joseph, like all Bellow's heroes, rapidly shifts perspective on his own life and on the world that surrounds him. The "self" has value at one moment and is meaningless the next, while the world is mooted as a place both to be clung to and to transcend.

Joseph's "quest" (p. 154), as he puts it, is to discover something that will "rescue us spiritually" (p. 168) and to this end he has turned himself inward. Interestingly, Joseph falls back on the "self" at a time when the goings-on in the outside world would seem to be most compelling. And yet Joseph regards the war against Hitler as a spiritual irrelevance, an "incident" that will "set us free in the crudest sense . . . to breathe and eat" but will not decide any of the "major issues of existence" (p. 168).

The major issue for Joseph centers on the amount of "pure freedom" (p. 154) that an individual can secure for himself in a world that is despotically deterministic. Like Albert Corde, Joseph is oppressed by political and social realities over which he has little or no control. But, Joseph has a stronger sense of his own worldly ineffectiveness. For Joseph, environment, family, and history all play a part in molding the individual and, to make matters worse, he feels that we are "afraid to govern ourselves." Given a grab at freedom we will "run out . . . choose a master, roll over on our backs and ask for the leash" (pp. 167–68). The bulk of *Dangling Man* charts Joseph's attempts to minimize the effects of formative influences upon his "self" and to assert the validity of his autonomous being. That he does so against the intellectual backdrop of his own belief in humankind's innate desire to be "leashed" is either a brave or a foolish thing. It is also an exemplary manifestation of Bellow's propensity to doom his heroes to long periods of knocking their heads against brick walls.

Oddly, it is not history in the shape of the Second World War that Joseph perceives as the greatest threat to his sense of self, but rather elements in his life that are closer to home: his extended family and his immediate environment. Joseph is particularly oppressed by his brattish niece, Etta. A spoiled little rich girl, Etta has all the confidence and manipulative power that the ego-less Joseph seems to lack. Nevertheless, in his "old" easygoing life, Joseph has made several attempts to make friends with her. Joseph's reason for these avuncular "advances" has been the uncanny physical resemblance that niece and uncle share. Believing that "a similarity of faces must mean a similarity of nature and presumably of fate" (p. 75), Joseph has plied Etta with his own favorite books and record albums. Predictably, Etta's response has been to treat her uncle with utter contempt, an attitude she has derived from her mother, Dolly—the first of Bellow's many female characters to judge a hero according to his income.

The "new" Joseph, who is self-protective and set on an autonomous life, conclusively decides that he and Etta "have nothing in common" (p. 78). What on the face of it has been merely a misreading of character on Joseph's part is, however, also a revelation of the "new" Joseph's deep need to rid himself of the stigma of familial influence. As a young man, Joseph tells us, he believed that his "face was the whole embodiment of [his] meaning:" He goes on:

> It was a register of my ancestors, a part of the world and, simultaneously, the way I received the world, clutched at it, and the way, moreover, in which I announced myself to it. (P. 76)

Joseph's face no longer holds such importance for him. Indeed it cannot, as he now wishes to deny the significance of heredity. Joseph is only the first of many Bellow heroes to be bothered by the notion that unpleasant family traits come in with the blood and cannot be forgone. More importantly, Joseph's two selves embody a salient characteristic of Bellow's later heroes: the need to identify with and yet be set apart from other members of the family. In *Dangling Man*, however, the issue of family influence is largely conducted theoretically, on an intellectual level. In later novels, it becomes more of an emotional issue— Augie March and Moses Herzog acting out, on a grander scale, Joseph's inner contradictions.

If Joseph is troubled by his family attachments, he is equally worried by the formative elements that he discovers in his environment. What to others is "merely neutral, the environment" (p. 153), is for Joseph something that contains "the difficult [and] the sorrowful" (ibid.). Walking the damp, dimly lit streets of his neighborhood or gazing through the window of his room at the black warehouses and garish neon signs that no snowfall can obliterate, Joseph begins to see the city of Chicago as a bleak map of the collective consciousness of its inhabitants.

> Where was there a particle of what, elsewhere or in the past, had spoken in man's favor. There could be no doubt that these billboards, streets, tracks, houses, ugly and blind, were related to interior life. (P. 24)

Reflexively, Joseph gives back to Chicago the "dark, burdensome" (p. 106) days that the city gives to him. In this double gloom, Joseph searches for some signs of an alternative reality, some confirmation that he and his fellow citizens are not "actually a reflection of the things they live[d] among" (p. 25):

> I tried continually to find clear signs of their [other people's] common humanity. . . .
> It was undeniably in my interest to do this. Because whether I liked it or not, they were my generation, my society, my world. We were figures in the same plot, eternally fixed together. I was aware, also, that their existence, just as it was, made mine possible. And if, as was often said, this part of the century was approaching the nether curve in a cycle, then I, too, would remain on the bottom there, extinct, merely add my body, my life, to the base of a coming time. (P. 25)

This is a central formulation in *Dangling Man* for it delineates the contours of Joseph's problem and explains his need to affirm a world in which there is (from his point of view) very little to affirm. Joseph must find a way to reconcile himself with his generation, society, and world because, although he would like to think differently, he believes that they are largely responsible for his "formation." An ugly world (like an ugly family) is more or less bound to bring about an ugly Joseph. It is therefore in Joseph's best interests to develop a more accommodating view of life on earth. However, in order to see the world in the way that he wants to, Joseph is obliged to deny the validity of his own perceptions. His situation seems hopeless.

Joseph's options are severely limited. Given that he can neither affirm nor deny either himself or the world that he inhabits, Joseph must either pray for the world to be magically transformed or find some way to transcend it. In 1942 those in the business of magically (or radically) transforming Joseph's America were mainly members of the Communist party. However, the local Chicago chapter of the Communist party has, we learn, lost Joseph's allegiance some ten years before his current crisis. As an impressionable eighteen year old, Joseph briefly flirted with revolutionary politics, but he soon came to the realization that "any hospital nurse did more with one bedpan for *le genre humain* than they [the Communist party] did with their entire organization" (p. 34).

Disillusioned with radical politics, Joseph has searched for other ways to "unlock the imprisoning self" (p. 153). His "role-model" in this endeavor is his artist-friend John Pearl. Pearl is a painter who maintains himself by working in an advertising agency at a job that he despises. He is, I believe, the only bona fide artist (of any kind) to crop up in Bellow's entire canon. The life that he leads and the ideas that he holds characterize him, rather stereotypically, as a kind of Yeatsian poet who has found his tower in a New York skyscraper and who is content to let his imagination scorn the earth. "The real world," Pearl writes to Joseph, "is the world of art and thought. There is only one worthwhile sort of work, that of the imagination" (p. 91). As far as Joseph is concerned, Pearl has "escaped a trap."

> There he is in New York, painting; and in spite of the calamity, the lies and the moral buggery, the odium, the detritus of wrong and sorrow dropped on every heart . . . he can keep a measure of cleanliness and freedom. (P. 91)

It is interesting that, given his propensity to mix fiction with autobiography, Bellow chose to make Joseph and not Pearl the central character of *Dangling Man*. It is as if the life of the artist as Bellow conceives it (or perhaps lives it?) has no energizing tension, no deep antithetical impulses, precisely because it is "transcendent" in the way that Joseph believes it to be. What always intrigues Bellow, and in this case also engages his hero, is the fate of the artistically talentless man who yet perceives the world through the eyes of an "outsider" artist. "But what about me?" Joseph asks:

> My talent, if I have one at all, is for being a good citizen, or what today is called most apologetically a good man. Is there some sort of personal effort that I can substitute for the imagination? (P. 91)

Joseph's substitute personal effort, I would suggest, is actually his journal. As he acknowledges on the opening page of the book, it is his daily writing that prevents him from becoming completely "demoralized" (p. 9). However, the "creative" writing of Bellow's heroes—we might think of Augie March's memoirs or Herzog's letters in the same category—is never allowed to appear as anything more than a series of aberrant, occasionally therapeutic jottings. Presumably, if a Bellow hero were to produce a serious work of the imagination, salvation would be his for the taking. However, unless Bellow decides to write a novel with an artist-hero, we cannot know for sure.

At one point in *Dangling Man,* we find Joseph "trimming [his] nails, listening absently" (p. 92) to his wife, who is searching for a lost copy of Joyce's *Dubliners.* The allusion to the aesthetically distanced artist in Joyce's *Portrait of the Artist as a Young Man* throws Joseph's own unaesthetic disengagement from the world into sharp relief. Interestingly, the concluding diary entries of *Portrait of the Artist* and *Dangling Man,* both made in April at the beginning of spring, offer a salutary contrast between the young Stephen cheerfully giving himself over to Art and the young Joseph capitulating, almost hysterically, to his demanding society. "Hurray for regular hours! And for the Supervision of the Spirit! Loing live regimentation!" (p. 191), cries Joseph, who has no expectations of forging anything grand or lasting in the smithy of his soul.

Joseph, then, is alienated from his society, but has neither Art nor the company of other artists to console him. Where John Pearl has "a community," Joseph has only a "six-sided box." Without a "substitute for the imagination," his situation is miserable.

> I, in this room, separate, distrustful, find in my purpose not an open world, but a closed hopeless jail. My perspectives end in walls. Nothing of the future comes to me. (P. 92)

As the weeks pass and the delay in his induction seems to stretch out interminably, Joseph's frustration with his own aimlessness rises to new levels of intensity. Unemployment and the "freedom" that it seemed to offer have turned his life into a nightmare. On his own admission Joseph has become intolerant and aggressive. Occasionally he boils over and becomes quite violent. In the course of the novel, he assaults his neighbor, Mr. Vanaker, punches his former landlord, Mr. Gesell, and spanks Etta!

Joseph's "unusual explosion[s] of temper" (p. 31), as he himself is aware, cannot wholly be attributed to the vacuum in his life that has been caused by his dangling between job and army. Something more fundamental to his being has risen to the surface in this period of enforced calm—something that Joseph is not altogether willing to confront. "Why do you quarrel with so many people?" asks Joseph's "Spirit of Alternatives," a kind of inner Dostoyevskian devil with whom Joseph occasionally communes. "Is it because they force you to recognize that you belong to their world?" (p. 138). Joseph answers himself evasively and the matter is dropped. However, throughout the novel, Joseph's violent behavior does indeed seem to be occasioned by what he conceives of as threats to his autonomy of self.

Two of Joseph's outbursts come about in the same way. Etta and Mr. Gesell both interrupt Joseph while he is listening to concert music, and on both occasions their interruptions are prelude to an assault by Joseph. In his "dangling" days, one of the few pleasures that remain to Joseph is the time that he spends alone playing his phonograph. He is particularly enamored of a Haydn divertimento that seems to have the power to lift him out of his misery and transport him to another world. The music, however, is in once sense problematic. For Joseph feels that Haydn's sober notes and Piatigorsky's resonating cello are manipulating him into a sense of irrational religious awe by penetrating the "seldom disturbed thickets around [his] heart" (p. 68).

As with everything else that threatens to take him over (history, family, environment), Joseph struggles to keep himself inviolate and not to give himself away to the music. The last thing that Joseph wants is to come away from his private concerts believing in God. His head has already pointed out the many ways in which he is not master of his own fate and he does not need his heart to start getting in on the act. Listening to

Haydn, Joseph wins what is perhaps his greatest victory, for ultimately he manages to take from the music what he wants and not what the music directs him to want. Unfortunately it is at the moments when he is feeling most triumphant—having imposed his autonomous mind on the moving forces of his heart and having, in fact, come closest to creating his own world—that Etta and Mr. Gesell choose to interrupt him.[1] Reminders of the interruptive, hostile reality that waits beyond the "music room," Etta and Gesell force Joseph to recognize that he "belongs to their world" (p. 138), and, as a result, he erupts.

Wherever he turns, the "freedom"-loving Joseph discovers himself to be formed, tied, inhibited, and limited. At the deepest level, his frustration and his anger are an expression of his dissatisfaction with the forms of daily life as he is required to live them. As Malcolm Bradbury has noted, Joseph's condition in many ways seems to be "explicitly 'existential,'" as Joseph is "not able to find essence in existence."[2] However, if Joseph is an American cousin to Sartre's Antoine Roquentin and Camus's Meursault, he is a cousin once removed. For, unlike the alienated heroes of *La Nausée* and *L'Etranger*, Joseph frequently takes time out to affirm the value of civilized life, to repudiate his own lapses into anomic despair and occasionally even to celebrate his threatening environment. Joseph's reasons for doing so (like Albert Corde's reasons for "affirming" life in America) are, however, all derived from a kind of "better of two evils" philosophy. For, perversely, Joseph turns out to be quite terrified of the "freedom" whose inaccessibility seems to be causing him so much trouble.

Even when Joseph take two small steps outside the "limiting" world that encircles him and begins an affair with a former Inter-American client he is quick to perceive the dangers. "A man must accept limits and cannot give in to the wild desire to be everyone and everything to everyone" (p. 101), Joseph explains to his mistress, Kitty Daumler, by way of terminating their two-month affair. Bellow's Joseph is clearly no Stephen Rojack. Indeed, he comes across to the reader as a young man who has struggled hard to keep not only his sexual but also his aggressive instincts in check. In marked contrast to the heroes of *L'Etranger* and Mailer's *An American Dream*, who perform symbolic liberating acts of murder and show no remorse, Joseph turns himself inside out and feels "disgraced" (pp. 59,

142) by his own comparatively mild and ineffective acts of violence.

Unlike what we might call the "authentic" existential hero, Joseph believes in the need for and value of a control that is both internal and external. "I do not like to think what we are governed by" (p. 83), he says, a generalization that he supports in his specific observations of some of the characters around him. For example, "working through" his mother-in-law, he finds "a malice she herself knew nothing about" (p. 22). Similarly, Joseph finds in his friend Morris Abt an equally unconscious propensity toward cruelty. Abt reveals his true nature at a party that Joseph unwillingly attends. Doing his "party-piece"—a demonstration of amateur hypnotism—Abt puts a drunk woman into a trance and then, to Joseph's dismay, begins to twist and pinch her skin until the blood drains out and large white blotches appear on her arm.

"Seeing through" others, Joseph has also begun to see through himself, and the "new" Joseph no longer believes "in his own mildness." Man, he decides, is "an animal who [has] to be tamed" (p. 39). Joseph, then, believes in the value of repression but is not always aware of the nature of his own repressions. For example, when Joseph spanks Etta for interrupting his concert, the act clearly suggests a measure of Joseph's sexual attraction for his niece; it suggests further that he has repressed it and that the repression has given rise to a mildly violent assault.

> I pulled her over my knee, trapping both her legs in mine. . . . "Don't you struggle," I cried, pressing her neck. . . . [H]er round, nubile thighs bare, lay in my lap. (P. 71)

A few pages earlier, Joseph has made a clear association between necks and vaginas (pp. 60–61), thus strengthening the links in the reader's mind between the spanking and the sexual act.

Through Joseph's observations on the behavior of others and, through the reader's observations, of Joseph's own behavior, it is clear that Joseph will not get his "freedom." For, as far as Joseph is concerned, to be governed by instinct—by the "malice" we know nothing about and do not wish to contemplate—is to risk opening a Pandora's box and creating a world even more intolerable than the one that he presently inhabits.

Moreover, thrown back on himself, Joseph's solipsistic imagination has only managed to produce a set of nightmarish visions. Viewing things "subjectively" from a "free" perspective, Joseph has become aware of just how thin the veil is that separates the ordered, civilized world from primeval chaos. Like Marlow's London in *Heart of Darkness,* Joseph's Chicago is imaged as a protean city, equally capable of revealing itself as "one of the dark places of the earth."

> Once more the horn bawled over the water, warning the late tugs from the headlands. It was not hard to imagine that there was no city here at all, and not even a lake but, instead, a swamp and that despairing bawl crossing it; wasting trees instead of dwellings, and runners of vine instead of telephone wires. (P. 96)

The brief glimpse that Joseph has of the city's dark underbelly (like his flashes of insight into the true nature of his friends and family) is enough to convince him that the real, objective world is worth another shot. Unlike the Dostoyevskian existential hero (Raskolnikov is a good example) who lives through and by his own subjective visions of the world, Joseph seeks an end to his isolation whenever his mind begins to wander free of its "objective" underpinnings. The oppressive environment— billboards; streets; tracks; houses, ugly and blind—of Joseph's objective world turns out to be not so bad after all. For, whatever its aesthetic failings, however strong its influence on "interior life," it performs a vital function in Joseph's life by diverting images of chaos.

Toward the end of *Dangling Man,* Joseph acknowledges that if he is not to go crazy he will have to trade in his autonomous imaginings for a set of safe and more commonly held views.

> I rose . . . feeling that there was an element of treason to common sense in the very objects of common sense. Or that there was no trusting them, save through wide agreement, and that my separation from such agreement had brought me perilously far from the necessary trust, auxiliary to all sanity. I had not done well alone. . . . To be pushed upon oneself entirely put the very facts of simple existence in doubt. (Pp. 190–91)

Joseph, indeed, does not do "well alone"—not nearly as well as all the solitary Bellovian heroes whom he anticipates. This is largely because Joseph, unlike Moses Herzog, does not know how to inflame himself with his own drama. And while his "dangling" is to become the prescriptive Bellovian mode of existence, his reaction to it is as yet unsophisticated.

At the end of *Dangling Man,* Joseph capitulates and joins the army. Resolved situations do not much interest Bellow and his first novel concludes where many other novels of the 1940s begin—on the hero's "last civilian day" (p. 191).

Fittingly, in his penultimate diary entry Joseph notes that he has received from his old antagonist Etta a going-away present consisting of "a leather sewing kit, complete with scissors and buttons" (p. 191). Throughout the novel Joseph's loose buttons have signalled his disengagement from the society he inhabits. He, too, dangles on a thread and his attempts to reattach himself are paralleled in his intermittent attempts to have his buttons sewn back on, only to find that his shirts come back from the laundry "without a single button" (p. 126). Etta, as always, represents the infringing and interfering world and her gift symbolically emphasizes Joseph's imminent reattachement (via the army) to the world he has sought to evade.

Some critics have seen *Dangling Man* as a great American war novel, evoking the home front and showing how distant battles altered the collective psyche. Others have found in Joseph's condition an objective correlative for the political atmosphere of the time.[3] Maxwell Geismar, writing in the 1950s, found that Joseph was able to summarize "almost too neatly the prevalent post-Marxist, nostalgically semi-religious American intellectual view of our modern dilemma."[4]

In all these versions, Joseph is viewed as something of a representative American man. I prefer to see him as most importantly a representative *Bellovian* man. Times have changed but the problems of Bellow's heroes have remained largely the same. It is not the war or the cold war that it anticipates that cause Joseph to dangle but, more profoundly, Bellow's overriding interest in the condition of a "dangling man" who is strung out on conflicts that seem to tear him apart, uncertain as to who he is, uncertain as to what the world is really like.

Dangling Man is a first novel, and because it is a first novel critics (myself included) have tended to search it for signposts to Bellow's later works. In many areas we *are* presented with Bellow's embryonic fictive universe. For example, the minor characters in *Dangling Man,* hardly developed at all, are nevertheless recognizable as the forebears of some of the members of Bellow's stock cast: wealthy brother—Amos; slovenly mistress—Kitty Daumler; charlatan/pseudophilosopher—Alf Steidler. However, where Joseph himself is concerned, it seems to me that we have much more than an "embryo." "Joseph's vitality as a *fictional* character is low," Ihab Hassan has noted; "the brilliant inventiveness of Bellow is still muted here, and the vigor of his imagination exhibits itself mainly in the dance of ideas."[5]

I would not dispute Professor Hassan's characterization of Joseph, but what interests me is why his "vitality" is low. I do not believe it can be ascribed to Bellow's youthful incapacity to create character, nor even, as Irving Malin would have us believe, to Bellow's failure to give Joseph a defining Jewish identity.[6] It is rather a condition of Joseph's dangling, and while Bellow does, in later novels, begin to flesh out his minor characters, his heroes remain inexorably characters whose substantial existence is always threatened by the very conflicts that give them life.

3

The Victim

The Victim belongs to that group of novels that, since the Romantic period, has thematically centered on "doubles," a combination of the hero and his "darker" self, who nevertheless assumes an autonomous personality. A "double" novel generically demands the kind of Manichaean confrontation in which Bellow delights. Moreover, to the fledgling novelist who in his first novel had chosen to be "confined" by the limitations of the diary form, the conventional limitations of a "double novel" must have seemed both a natural progression and a liberation. As Keith Opdahl was the first to note, Leventhal and Allbee, respectively the hero and "double" of *The Victim,* "play out the split that Joseph suffers in his room."[1] However, with two opposing central characters instead of a single personality turned against itself, Bellow was able to turn the novel on a broader axis.

Leventhal is a youngish trade journalist, a hack; happily married (by Bellovian standards) and living in Manhattan. Initially, Bellow stresses Leventhal's ordinariness: the range of his intellect and the limits of his needs and desires seeming to conform perfectly with his middle-class, middle-income status. However, as Leventhal's character develops, it becomes clear that if he is a "representative man," it can only be of that group of inner-city dwellers who have become sensitive to the point of paranoia and whose character is defined by fear and mistrust. Like Joseph in *Dangling Man*'s "old self," Leventhal senses the world as hostile but struggles to convince himself that it is, after all, accommodating.

Kirby Allbee, Leventhal's intrusive, irresistible "double" is one of the most convincing and least endearing of Bellow's "cranks." A former commercial journalist himself, Allbee turns up out of nowhere to accuse Leventhal of having, with malicious intent, lost him a job some three years previously. Allbee is

53

an unpleasant, abusive anti-Semite who preaches darkness and misery for the human race. Indeed, he expounds a deterministic philosophy bleaker even than that of Joseph's "new self." While Leventhal and Allbee play out Joseph's intellectual "split," they are not in themselves intellectual characters. Leventhal clearly lacks the kind of "reading" knowledge that sustains and enlivens Joseph, while Allbee's twisted behavior effectively precludes any consideration of him as a serious thinker.

Asa Leventhal is, in fact, one of only two Bellow heroes to lack a sophisticated capacity to consolidate his thoughts into language—the other being Tommy Wilhelm in *Seize the Day*. However, as if to compensate Leventhal for his intellectual shortcomings, Bellow has given him a powerful and palpable physical presence in the novel. The burly Leventhal with his large head and huge childlike eyes makes up in the body for what he lacks in the mind—and the same is true of the hippopotamic Wilhelm. Moreover, in *The Victim*, as in *Seize the Day*, the central character embodies values that are tested in action rather than in echoing caverns of the mind.

In his book *On Moral Fiction*, John Gardner argues that Saul Bellow is "not actually a novelist at heart but an essayist disguised as a writer of fiction." Even in those novels where Bellow makes "serious use of fictional techniques," he says, "the essayist-lecturer is always ready to step in, stealing the stage from the fictional characters to make the fiction more 'important.'" Gardner's criticism is largely prescriptive and the parameters of his ideal fiction are narrow and exclusive. However, his analysis of Bellow, whom he refers to as an "old-fashioned modern,"[2] raises some important issues with regard to *The Victim*.

For Gardner, the great weakness of Bellow's fiction is his tendency to subordinate the substantiation and interaction of characters to lengthy segments of discursive thought—"Bellow leans his characters on some door frame, turns off his fiction's clock, and, from behind the mask of hero expatiates."[3] While this may be true of Bellow's other novels, it certainly cannot be said of *The Victim*. For one thing, Asa Leventhal would not be credible as a mouthpiece for Bellow, and for another, Bellow's modes of characterization in *The Victim* closely conform to the kind of standards that have earned him the reputation of a "traditional novelist." According to Gardner's prescriptions, *The Victim* (which, oddly, he does not mention in his essay) should come across as Bellow's most successful work of fiction.

However, the effect on Bellow's fiction of his decision to create "personalities" rather than "minds" is profound. For, when Bellow abandons his intellectual heroes along with the "long passages of discursive thought," he lays down some of the strongest weapons in his fictive arsenal: the darting wit, shrewd observation, and entertaining speculation that his brilliant monologuists always carry with them as part of their mental baggage. The fat men, Leventhal and Wilhelm, who occasionally turn up in Bellow's novels, point up what is an unresolved dilemma in Bellow's canon. For, the almost literal "thickening" of fictional texture that Bellow gains when he enters what we might call a simpler mind than his own is purchased at great expense.

For all its "thickened" central characters and despite Bellow's introduction of a convincing set of minor characters, *The Victim* seems, if anything, an even more claustral work than its predecessor.

The novel opens with an image of Manhattan that, like one of Joseph's visions of Chicago, transforms the city into a chaotic, primeval place.

> On some nights New York is as hot as Bangkok. The whole continent seems to have moved from its place and slid nearer the equator, the bitter grey Atlantic to have become green and tropical, and the people, thronging the streets, barbaric fellahin among the stupendous monuments of their mystery. . . . (P. 3)

These powerful and evocative images soon merge with more conventional descriptions of New York during a long hot summer. The city becomes familiarly oppressive, its atmosphere stifling; its inhabitants, alien and hostile, especially when we apprehend them in large silent masses traveling on the subway or the Staten Island ferry. Against this background—every bit as threatening and alienating as Joseph's uninhabitable Chicago or Corde's Bucharest—Bellow lays down a plot which, appropriately, centers on "illness, madness and death" (p. 158).

Leventhal is spending the summer alone in New York. His wife Mary is out of town helping her mother move. Somewhat helpless in the style of a "fifties" bachelor, Leventhal is also busy feeling abandoned and sorry for himself. His troubles are multiplied by the fact that his brother, Max, whom Leventhal regards as highly irresponsible, has taken off to find work in

Texas. Much to his annoyance Leventhal is obliged to assume some of the burden of his brother's family. When we are first introduced to him he has just returned from a visit to his sister-in-law, Elena, who has a sick child on her hands and is beside herself with worry.

Sickness, madness, and hysteria are on Leventhal's mind when Allbee steps into his path and Leventhal's real trials begin. During their initial confrontation, all that Allbee wishes is to accuse. Leventhal, he claims, was not only instrumental in losing him his job (Bellow never makes clear whether he was or wasn't), but was also responsible for his divorce and the subsequent death of his wife in a road accident. Later he demands that Leventhal make reparations, although the form they are to take remains unspecified until late in the novel.

Bellow, apparently quite without consciousness of what he was doing, borrowed the plot of *The Victim* from Dostoevski's novella *The Eternal Husband.* As "doubles," Leventhal and Allbee in many ways parallel Velchaninov and Pavel Pavlovich, the "doubles" in the Dostoevski story, but the conflict they enact is substantially different.[4] The Dostoevski story treats fairly lightly the relationship between two men who have loved the same woman—her husband (now widower) and a former lover. The two characters move, like Leventhal and Allbee, from hostility to reconciliation. However, the grounds of their hostility remain centered on the jealousy surrounding their relationships with the woman. In *The Victim,* the central point of the two characters' conflict is derived from Allbee's anti-Semitism; and while anti-Semitism does not seem to me to be the central *theme* of *The Victim* it is a vital element in establishing and altering the relationship between the two central figures.

In the conventional manner of a "double" work, Allbee and Leventhal's surface differences are stressed: Allbee is a gentile, Leventhal a Jew; Allbee is fair and Leventhal dark; Allbee is descended from old American stock (Governor Winthrop) while Leventhal is the child of Russian-Jewish immigrants. However, their affinities are more subtly conveyed. Leventhal, we learn, has come close to experiencing Allbee's near-total impoverishment; he scorns Allbee's drinking but toward the end of the novel gets drunk himself; and most significantly there is a strong homoerotic element in the relationship between the two men.

It is, however, on the level of their ideas that Allbee and

Leventhal come closest to "repeating" one another, with Allbee drawing conclusions that Leventhal seems too timid to reach. Leventhal perceives the world as hostile, but imagines that, to a certain extent, one may control one's own fate in it; Allbee agrees that the world is hostile—a place where men "get it in the neck for nothing" (p. 146)—but is also convinced, as he tells Leventhal, that it is a place where the individual has little or no control over his own destiny.

> You don't agree that people have destiny forced on them? Well that's all the destiny they get, so they'd better not assume they're running their own show. (P. 71)

If Leventhal's starting point is bleak, the alternatives, as outlined by Allbee are bleaker. Indeed, in company with Allbee, Leventhal does appear something of an "everyman" if only because he represents the positive side of his antagonist's "all be."

In *Dangling Man,* the selfish and egotistic characters who surround Joseph give credence to his development of a despairing vision of the world. In *The Victim,* however, Leventhal's and Allbee's cheerless apprehensions are partly offset by the presence of a set of minor characters whose vision is of a more accommodating world. Through their voices, the novel seems to "officially" affirm the existence and validity of a fairly pleasant, harmonious world. Yet, *The Victim* fails to consolidate either in plot or atmosphere the congenial versions of reality that the minor characters endorse.

Significantly, positive characters chimerically appear on the periphery of the novel, and do not effectively qualify it. Like Leventhal's wife Mary, or his brother Max, or his friend Harkavy, they are honest, genial, generous types, who are adjusted to a world that they find neither unbearably despotic nor inescapably deterministic. In the extreme case they even philosophize about the possibility of accommodation to the world. Thus, the most substantial and significant representative of this group is the old Yiddish journalist Schlossberg, who pontificates on these issues. His advice to Leventhal and an assorted company, not to try to be more than human and not to allow oneself to become "less than human" (p. 133) is typical of his philosophy. Schlossberg posits the acceptance of human limitation as an essential prerequisite for the discovery of meaning in life, and for the achievement of a solid identity. But Schlossberg's philosophy, which implies acceptance of life's hardships, and the behavior of characters like Max who demonstrate such resilience, hardly dominate the novel.

Quite the contrary. Bellow suggests that the world may not be as Leventhal or Allbee see it. Yet, what in fact is it like? If we look at the environment of *The Victim* as Joseph looks at his environment in *Dangling Man,* we are hard put, like Joseph, to find "a particle . . . of what speaks in man's favor" (*Dangling Man,* p. 24). The affirmations of Schlossberg et al. are made to appear as empty as those of Joseph's "old self." For, if Leventhal's darkest perceptions are offset by those of his friends and relatives, they are more than consolidated by the atmosphere of despondence that hangs over the novel and by the plot, which has to do with the death of Leventhal's nephew, Leventhal's own fears of mental illness, and, centrally, Allbee's vicious persecution of Leventhal.

Bleakly, *The Victim* offers us no kind of reassurance that the world imagined by the fearful and suspicious Leventhal is any different from the "real" world that he inhabits. Leventhal and Allbee do not represent Bellow's only "double vision" in the novel. For, while Bellow distances himself and the reader from Leventhal's and Allbee's "distortions" of reality, he simultaneously takes pains to reinforce some of their uglier presentiments. The first hints of this overlapping of "subjective" and "objective" worlds come when we realize that Leventhal's disfiguring visions of New York are not too different from those provided by Bellow's third-person narrator.

As Leventhal's crises deepen, he begins to see Manhattan in much the same light that Joseph, in his most desperate moments, saw Chicago.

> The towers on the shore rose up in huge blocks, scorched smoky, grey and bare and white where the sun was direct upon them. The notion brushed Leventhal's mind that the light over them and over the water was akin to the yellow revealed in the slit of the eye of a wild animal, say a lion, something inhuman that didn't care about anything human and yet was implanted in every human being too, one speck of it. . . . (P. 51)

As if this were not bad enough, Leventhal's transfiguring vision of primordial light turns out to be merely an auroral glow off the infernal city. Taking respite from his troubles on a park bench and observing his fellow New Yorkers at play, Leventhal is moved to bring to mind a soul-chilling image of "Hell cracking open . . . and all the souls, crammed together, looking out" (p. 184).

However, the narrator's descriptions, hard to separate from Leventhal's own, seem to consolidate rather than deny Leventhal's own insights. Tricks of light, the evocative heat, shadows of huge buildings, and monumental silhouettes combine to create an atmosphere quite as primordial and infernal as any that Leventhal imagines. Symbolically, Leventhal's journeys in the novel, on foot, by subway, or on the Staten Island ferry, seem to take him back in time, or down into a Dantesque netherworld, or into a jungle. But, we are never sure if it is Leventhal or reality itself that is causing the solid landmarks of Leventhal's daily life to melt into ghostly, hellish apparitions.

It is Leventhal's experiences with Allbee, however, that suggest most powerfully that, like Joseph in *Dangling Man,* he is trapped between equally unpleasant "real" and "imagined" worlds.

At their first meeting, before even a word has passed between them, Leventhal is prepared to punch Allbee because he has walked toward him looking suspicious. As their conversation progresses and Allbee becomes increasingly bitter and hostile, Leventhal inwardly prepares himself to "punch him in the jaw . . . throw him down and smash his ribs for him" (p. 35). Leventhal's own violent disposition imaginatively matches Allbee's vituperative outbursts. While it is made clear in the novel that Leventhal is paranoid and tends to overreact to provocation, it is also suggested that the kind of unmotivated and unexpected violence that can be unleashed upon an individual in the city is a commonplace rather than exceptional. Leventhal may be paranoid, Bellow seems to be saying, but he has something to be paranoid about. While Allbee, to begin with, is only verbally abusive, the compulsive and unpredictable manner in which he bursts into and disrupts Leventhal's life is suggestive of the larger and equally unfathomable, violent eruptions that punctuate city life, and to which Leventhal is occasional witness.

Gradually Allbee begins to infiltrate Leventhal's life, arriving uninvited at Leventhal's apartment, or embarrassingly showing up at Leventhal's office, or coincidentally bumping into him at the zoo. The peripatetic Allbee will not let Leventhal forget

him. The paradox at the heart of *The Victim* is slowly revealed to
us through the transformation of Leventhal's character after
his first confrontation with Allbee. Understandably Leventhal
is repelled by Allbee, by both his behavior and what he has to
say: Allbee is demanding, insinuating, and full of anti-Semitic
jibes. However, Leventhal is also drawn to him, first intellectually, and then, as slowly becomes clear, emotionally. As their
meetings begin to lengthen and their conversations to expand,
we realize that Leventhal is fascinated by Allbee partly because
he confirms his own worst suspicions as to the nature of human
life. Whatever Leventhal feels to be the case but is unwilling to
admit, Allbee will vociferously protest. "This self-made business [is] bunk,'" Allbee tells Leventhal, "it's all blind movement,
vast movement, and the individual is shuttled back and forth"
(p. 70). Deep down, we know this to be what Leventhal secretly
believes—but it is hardly music to his ears.

Faced with a man whose vision of the world (partly because it
is articulated) is even harsher and more pessimistic than his
own, Leventhal performs a kind of ideological turnabout. As
Allbee's depressing insights proliferate, Leventhal begins to
affirm tentatively the value, harmony, and essential benevo-
lence of the world that he inhabits. But, when out of Allbee's
presence, he quickly reverts to his own negative misgivings
about the world. Significantly, Leventhal embodies one of the
governing characteristics of those Bellow heroes who tend to
define themselves through opposition. Experiencing a horrible
persecution that should only confirm that his paranoia is
clearsightedness, Leventhal argues with his persecutor that the
world is better than he thinks it is.

If Allbee's behavior precipitates an affirmative reaction in
Leventhal, it also acts as a catalyst to his achieving a new clarity
of perception. A week after Allbee's first appearance, Leventhal witnesses an unpleasant scene on the street outside his
apartment. Towards dawn he is awakened by a woman's
scream. He draws the curtains in time to see a man rushing
crazily at two shrieking women, while two soldiers casually look
on. Leventhal is provoked to muse that he really does not know
what "strange, savage things" go on around him.

> They hung near him all the time in trembling drops, invisible
> usually, or seen from a distance. But that did not mean that
> there was always to be a distance, or that sooner or later one
> or two of the drops might not fall on him. (P. 94)

Like Joseph, Leventhal believes that he lives on the edge of chaos; disaster is around every corner, the civilized world inhabited by everyday, conative individuals like Leventhal can, within the space of a moment, be transformed into a terrifying place. However, *chaos* appears to have a far wider range of meaning for Leventhal than it does for Joseph. For, Leventhal seems to have established a fixed set of borders that he is afraid to cross, borders that are both social and psychological and that separate the elements of order in his life from those of chaos.

In social terms, Leventhal is scared of falling back into the "class" of people who are jobless and destitute—"the outcast, the overcome, the effaced, the ruined" (p. 20). Indeed, although the novel is set in the immediate postwar period, Leventhal's fears clearly have their roots in the Depression.

In terms of his psyche, Leventhal is equally afraid of falling into a "nether" world. With his wife out of town and with Allbee driving him crazy, Leventhal's latent aggressive instincts and sexual desires are put to the test. Bellow makes it clear that Leventhal is troubled by what might happen were he to let himself go. Moreover, Leventhal is obsessed with his mother's insanity; terrified that it may be hereditary; and, worried that the madness may already be in him, he remains constantly on the watch for signs of its emergence. Destitution, "instinctual" behavior, and madness are all synonymous with "chaos" in Leventhal's inner world.

Leventhal considers himself "lucky" to have managed to stay on the right side of the line separating the blessed from the damned. This sense of an abyss that one may easily tumble into were it not for "luck" also accompanies Moses Herzog and Eugene Henderson. In *Dangling Man* and *The Victim* as in *Herzog* and *Henderson the Rain King,* the hero is permitted glimpses of a reality that co-exists with his own and that he is "lucky" not to have become a part of. In all cases, these glimpses are enough to convince the hero of his good fortune in inhabiting a world that, although he may find it unbearable, is preferable to its alternative. Bellow's heroes are thus constantly obliged to adapt to a world that they find unaccommodating in preference to the risk of falling into the hellish world that waits for them with open gates.

Leventhal, who during a brief period of unemployment spent some time in a sleazy hotel on lower Broadway, is ever mindful of the fate that he has escaped. But the world that he "happily" inhabits is, for him, an alien, oppressive place, full of

vindictive individuals plotting conspiracies. Leventhal believes
that Allbee can have him blacklisted, although his friend Harkavy tells him that this is nonsense; he believes that his brother
Max's mother-in-law hates him and holds him responsible for
her grandchild's sickness, although his brother Max tells him it
is nonsense; he believes that his ten-year-old nephew holds a
nameless grudge against him; he even comes to believe that his
wife (one of Bellow's nicer women) may be deceiving him—an
idea maliciously, and easily, fostered in his head by Allbee. Leventhal's world is one in which all loyalties are unsure.

To make matters worse, as if its inhabitants were not antagonistic enough, New York City itself seems to have animated its
environment in order to pressure the pressured Leventhal still
further. Like a character in a comic silent movie, he is attacked
by maleficent machines: personified subway cars who slam their
doors shut on Leventhal and "flee," or trucks that "encircle"
him. Even Leventhal's own clothing seems to have a life of its
own, constricting him, resisting him to the point where even his
getting dressed seems a violent engagement with yet another
"self." It is no wonder that Leventhal feels his life to be an
"unremitting daily fight" (p. 285).

Perhaps the most devastating effects of civilized life upon
Leventhal are those achieved by forces of which he is only
partly conscious. Feeling, as he does, that he is in conflict with a
world that he has no choice but to affirm, Leventhal has stored
up an enormous amount of resentment. Leventhal knows that
the netherworld where "cannibalistic things" (p. 99) are done, is
a place that recognizes no limits, where people are defined by
their very refusal to curb the instincts that Leventhal struggles
to keep in check. Time and again in the novel we witness Leventhal holding back. Forever promising to himself that he will
"smash Allbee's ribs," or the like (p. 35) he always ends up by
merely pushing him. In fact, the only physical harm that Leventhal ever causes Allbee is the result of an accident.

None of this would matter if Bellow did not make so much of
the harmful "side-effects" of Leventhal's restraint. Unable to
find an outlet in action, Leventhal's aggressive instincts are
turned in on himself with disastrous consequences.

> He felt that . . . his rage had done him harm, affected his very
> blood. He had an impression of bad blood as something
> black, thick, briny, caused by sickness or lust or excessive
> anger. (P. 148)

Essentially, this is the fate that Bellow prescribes for all of his heroes who are done unto but who cannot bring themselves to take revenge. The cuckolded Moses Herzog who has murder in his heart knows all about "balked longings coming back as stinging poison," coming back, in fact, much as they do to Asa Leventhal.

> He felt as though something terrible, inflammatory, bitter, had been grated into his bloodstream and stung and burned his veins, his face, his heart . . . he now grasped the floating suspicion that this poison rose from within. (*Herzog,* pp. 230–31)

The vital difference between Herzog and Leventhal is the inability of the latter to draw the sting of his tribulations by, as Herzog puts it, "changing it all into language" (*Herzog,* p. 272). The floating suspicion that Herzog grasps is soon transformed into an idea, intellectualized, and thus, as far as Herzog is concerned, defused. The duller Leventhal, who can neither act on his instincts, nor accept the world in which he is confined, *nor* "change it all into language," is doomed to be crucified on his own inner conflicts.

Norman Podhoretz, writing in one of his preconservative incarnations, found *The Victim* to be an "oppressive" novel because it displayed "a pessimism over the human condition even darker than Freud's in *Civilization and Its Discontents.*" For Leventhal, says Podhoretz, "the making of a settlement (that is, the stifling of the instincts) is seen as bringing no positive rewards or compensations of any significance . . . it merely has the negative virtue of preventing the outbreak of 'cannibalism.' "[5]

In *The Victim* Bellow images the dialectical opposition of Civilization and its Discontents in what are Manichaean, theological terms. Those who refuse to acknowledge limits on their behavior, like Allbee, or those who get "fed up" with the orthodoxy of the rat race and try to break free, like a whore Leventhal sees fighting on the street, have, as Leventhal puts it, "signed on with the Devil and what they called the powers of darkness" (p. 99).

Significantly, minor characters whose vindictive behavior or competitive hostility seems to go beyond the bounds of the norm are "tinged" hellishly red. Rudiger, Allbee's former employer and perhaps the most unpleasant character in the novel, is, as his name suggests, "broad featured and red" with hair that

is "intensely red" (p. 42). His overly aggressive personality recalls for the reader a figure whom Leventhal has made note of
at a Fourth of July office picnic, a "man with red hair who
struggled forward [in the three-legged race] angry with his
partner, as if the race were a pain and a humiliation which he
could wipe out only by winning" (p. 15). In this company Leventhal comes across not so much as merely "civilized" but as
perversely angelic. As his friend Harkavy tells him, "Asa, we're
not children. We're men of the world. It's almost a sin to be so
innocent" (p. 88). Joseph in *Dangling Man*'s semihumorous
characterization of men as the "feeble-minded children of
angels" (p. 137), is always pertinent to a discussion of the
characterization of Bellow's heroes.

Leventhal's civilized "angelicism" is further put to the test by
the prolonged absence of his wife. "A bachelor for a month"
(p. 151), he never consciously contemplates an affair, but the
reader is made aware of his unconscious desires. As John Jay
Clayton has pointed out, Leventhal "gets rid of his guilt by
projecting these desires onto Kirby Allbee."[6] When Leventhal
descends in an elevator "amid a crowd of girls from the commercial school upstairs," he is "largely unconscious of the pleasure that he took in their smooth arms and smooth faces"
(p. 175), but when he and Allbee share the same elevator, the
latter is less reticent. "Nice," Allbee whispers. "Nice little tender
things. Soon you and I will be too old to take notice" (p. 200).
As Leventhal's double, it is Allbee's "job" to make manifest and
articulate Leventhal's hidden impulses. Leventhal does his best
not to acknowledge the truth of what Allbee has to say—but
Bellow does not let him get away with it. Late in the novel, a
brief episode makes it quite clear what has been going on in
Leventhal's mind while his wife has been away at her mother's.

Gradually reducing his hostility toward Albee, Leventhal has
permitted him to move into his apartment for a short period.
Abusing his hospitality, Allbee brings a woman back while Le-
venthal is out. When Leventhal returns home unexpectedly
Allbee refuses to open the door, and the impatient and angry
Leventhal throws himself at it and breaks the chain.

There Allbee, naked and ungainly, stood beside a woman
who was dressing in great haste. . . . She had on her skirt but
from the waist up she was bare. . . . Her hair covered her
face; nevertheless Leventhal thought he recognized her. Mrs.

Nunez! Was it Mrs. Nunez? The horror of it bristled on him, and the outcry he had been about to make was choked down. (P. 269)

Mrs. Nunez is Leventhal's superintendent's wife, and throughout the novel Leventhal has felt a certain sexual suggestiveness emanating from her. Discovering Allbee in his apartment with a seminaked woman, Leventhal gives rein to his own sexual fantasy. However, as he soon discovers, the woman is not Mrs. Nunez. Nevertheless, "the horror" that Leventhal feels is as if he himself had committed an adulterous act. When he discovers his error, he is "enormously lightened" (p. 269), but "it gave him a pang to think of his suspicion" (p. 270).

Arriving after Leventhal's wife has departed and departing before she returns, Allbee is a convenient outlet for Leventhal's self-loathing, something that we may legitimately interpret is in part derived from both his disgust at his own sexual desires that have surfaced in his wife's absence and from his fear at what the transformation of such impulses into action may bring. Leventhal's "bad blood" is caused, we will remember, among other things, by *lust*. Allbee's behavior in the novel allows Leventhal to mitigate some of the consequences of holding this "lust" in check, by giving him an opportunity to turn his aggression inside out. Allbee as "dark self" is also a projected self, sometimes a personified animus and sometimes a diabolic, surrogate wife or mistress, stroking Leventhal's hair, or mysteriously entering and leaving his apartment so that the building's superintendent suspects that Leventhal has a lover.

With so many important elements of his being embodied in another character, it is hardly surprising that Leventhal often feels as if he does not really occupy his own personality. Moreover, struggling, like Joseph, to keep himself inviolate and to achieve some minimal measure of control over his own destiny, Leventhal has become obsessed, again like Joseph, with the notion that large sections of his psyche have been formed for him. Leventhal is preoccupied with his late mother's insanity and openly voices the fear that heredity has played a dirty trick on him. He "dread[s] the manifestation of anything resembling [his mother's madness] in himself" (p. 53), and the extent of his dread is formidable.

When Harkavy, concerned about the inroads that Allbee is making into Leventhal's life, asks with some concern

"What are you letting this man do to you? Are you going off
your rocker?" Leventhal replies "Don't be foolish, Dan. I
know you mean well but you're being carried away. And
please remember my mother before you say a thing like
that." (P. 263)

A sense of Leventhal's fear of maternal "influence" is reinforced by the disproportionately aggressive manner in which
he treats anyone with whom he identifies his mother. In particular, Leventhal is quick to draw a parallel between his dis-
traught sister-in-law, Elena, and the behavior of his mentally
unstable parent. In Leventhal's view, Elena not only behaves
like "any parent with a sick child" (p. 54), but also like Leventhal's mother, which means that she acts like a mad woman. In
turn, this guarantees that Leventhal's responses to her will be
mainly those of an angry or confused child.

In his obsession with the potentially damaging formative influences of a parent, Leventhal prefigures Augie March, whose
engagement with the world is largely concentrated in his relationships with surrogate parent figures; and Tommy Wilhelm
(*Seize the Day*) whose struggles with his father, and all that he
represents, dominate the novella in which he appears.

For Leventhal, his mother's madness is yet another latent
"chaotic" element in his being. As, above all else, he does not
wish to be a man whose personality is governed by madness,
aggression, or sexual desire, the question arises as to how Leventhal can secure an identity for himself while accepting limitations on his behavior and imposing limitations on the wild
paranoia of his psyche.

In *Dangling Man,* Joseph, if not Bellow, suggests that it is only
through Art that a man may transcend the squalor of daily life
and yet "maintain himself," have an idea of who he is (*Dangling
Man,* p. 91). Unfortunately for Joseph, he is not an artist and
thus considers himself doomed to a lifetime of frustration. In
The Victim, the old Yiddish journalist Schlossberg fulfills the
role vacated by the artist John Pearl in *Dangling Man.* Schlossberg too has ideas on how to secure an identity and remain at
peace with the world. During a café conversation with some of
his cronies, to which Leventhal is witness, he notes the current
trend towards dissolution of the self.

"My mother sewed her own shroud," said Kaplan. . . . "All the
old people used to do it. And a good custom, too, don't you

think so Mr. Schlossberg." "There's a lot to say for it," Schlossberg replied. "At least they knew where they stood and who they were, in those days. Now they don't know who they are but they don't want to give themselves up." (P. 255)

Positing ethnicity as a strong factor in securing identity, Schlossberg's words have some relevance for Leventhal. Throughout the novel Leventhal adamantly defends an ethnic position that seems to have no defining effect whatsoever upon his identity. Leventhal is one of those who, not knowing who he is, nevertheless refuses to "give [him]self up." He feels constantly threatened, but is unsure as to what exactly it is in him that is being threatened. He defends Jews against the anti-Semitic Allbee, but his own Jewishness fails to provide him with any kind of self-assurance.

As a remedy, Schlossberg suggests not a return to Orthodox Judaism, but the development of a healthy respect for limits and an awareness of death that will symbolically enable one to retain a sense of proportion as to what can be achieved in a single lifetime. To "concentrate" a life rather than to dissolve it, is his message.

"There's a limit to me. But I have to be myself in full. Which is somebody who dies, isn't it? That's what I was from the beginning. I'm not three people, four people. I was born once and will die once. You want to be two people? More than human? Maybe it's because you don't know how to be one. . . . (P. 255)

To be "oneself" is to be "human" and to be human is to attach certain values to life.

"I am as sure about greatness and beauty as you are about black and white. If a human life is a great thing to me, it *is* a great thing. Do you know better? I'm entitled as much as you. And why be measly? Do you have to be? Is somebody holding you by the neck? Have dignity, you understand me. Choose dignity. Nobody knows enough to turn it down." (P. 134)

If Leventhal is afraid of "freedom" in the form of madness, released instincts, and all the other elements of chaos that "freedom" seems to correspond to here as in Bellow's other novels, then perversely, he seems almost indifferent to "limita-

tion." Schlossberg offers to secure Leventhal an identity if he
will submit to stricter limits on his life. But Schlossberg's admo-
nitions (like John Pearl's advice to Joseph) fall on deaf ears. Just
as Leventhal is obliged to deny Allbee's arguments, so too is he
incapable of accepting Schlossberg's. Unsure as to who he himself is, Leventhal tends to define himself only in opposition.
This form of definition is especially prevalent among Bellow's
early heroes and reaches its purest form in *The Adventures of
Augie March*. However, unlike Augie, who is aware of (and
proud of) his propensity to generate the categories of his personality in opposition to the defining categories of those who
surround him, Leventhal opposes but at the same time enormously resents those who oppose him.

Leventhal is thus revealed as one of Bellow's most painfully
rent "dangling men." Terrified of the "free," chaotic world that
exists in repressed state in his being and that manifests itself
visibly in his society, Leventhal is, at the same time, incapable of
shoring up his identity by accepting the limits that both he and
society place on his life. Leventhal can neither accept himself
for who and what he is nor find a means of expressing his
"pain" and thus alleviating it. He certainly cannot, as Bellow's
later heroes do, come to terms with the contradictions in his
own personality. Leventhal remains unable to resolve his dilemma by committing himself to either "chaos" or "order."

Toward the end of the novel, Allbee tries to gas himself in
Leventhal's apartment (in what Leventhal later calls "a suicide
pact without getting my permission first" (p. 286). Leventhal
awakes in the nick of time and discovers Allbee; as they struggle
on the floor, Allbee cries "Me, myself! . . . Me!" (p. 283). The
ambiguous cry and the fight itself at once stress Leventhal's
detachment from and attachment to Allbee. Leventhal is wrestling not only with the obnoxious, pathetic Allbee but also with
his own devil and all that that devil stands for. Leventhal's
triumph in the struggle signals his release from Allbee's persecution and from his painful struggle with his own dark instincts
and darker premonitions about life. However, the world into
which Leventhal is symbolically reborn is one in which he is still
somewhat governed by paranoid fears and oppressed by daily
"reality."

In the *coda* to the novel, we meet Leventhal "a few years"
(p. 285) after his dramatic conflict with Allbee. But a sense of

his having learned something from his experience is hardly
conveyed. As Tony Tanner has written,

> Bellow does not really show us a changed and wiser man so
> much as merely a more confident, less neurotic man.[7]

Allbee too has come through, and when we finally see him and
Leventhal together, as they meet by chance at a theater, the
initial roles in which we discovered them have been reversed.
Early in the novel Allbee has told Leventhal:

> "When I compare myself with you, why you're in the empy-
> rean, as they used to say at school, and I'm in the pit." (P. 69)

At the end of the novel we find an apparently wealthy Allbee
occupying a theater box with a beautiful, if faded, movie star;
while Leventhal heads for the stalls with his heavily pregnant
wife.

The Victim is a complex work. Extravagantly praised for its
moral perspicacity—Diana Trilling, at the time of the novel's
publication, called it "morally one of the farthest-reaching
books our contemporary culture has produced"—it has also
received adverse criticism for the dim view of human life that it
seems to present. Aside from Norman Podhoretz, whose negative misgivings I have already cited, Maxwell Geismar felt that
Leventhal's "paranoia, madness . . . guilt, anxiety and fear"
contributed to a novel altogether "lacking in warmth, humor
and joy." Argument as to *The Victim*'s central theme has also
been wide-ranging; for some critics, like Leslie Fiedler, the
novel is "Bellow's book about anti-Semitism," while for others,
like Malcolm Bradbury and John Jay Clayton, such concerns
are peripheral to the novel's larger philosophic explorations of
the nature and limits of personal responsibility.[8]

A highly concentrated work—Bellow himself felt the novel to
be in the tradition of Flaubert and "tried to make it letter perfect"[9]—the extent of conscious design in the novel is immediately apparent. Names have an overt symbolic or allegorical function, two main lines of imagery—connected to water
and to the theater—are apparent throughout, and thematically
Bellow reinforces his plot and subplot. However, as Keith Opdahl has pointed out, despite (or perhaps because of) the ex-

tent of Bellow's artistic contrivance, critics have been hard put
to determine "what *The Victim* is about. . . ."

> Bellow had created living characters in a brilliantly evoked
> physical world . . . but he hadn't told a clear story. He had
> designed a plot to overcome the obscurity of *Dangling Man*
> but for some reason had failed.[10]

With the aid of hindsight, and seen in the terms of Bellow's
entire canon to date, *The Victim* appears less obscure. Its themes
are essentially those of all Bellow's novels. Its hero, like all the
heroes, is a "dangling man" trapped in what are for him impossible situations. Leventhal remains an unusual Bellow hero, un-
reliable as a window on the world, he is, in addition, incapable
of mediating the terms of his own perceptions. Nevertheless,
his predicament is the common one.

As Bellow himself has revealed, after he wrote *The Victim* he
grew tired of the self-imposed "Flaubertian standard" that he
had striven to meet in his first two novels.[11] The standard was
"repressive" and Bellow began to feel that he had more to lose
than to gain from trying to conform to tasteful notions of literary correctness.

If we return briefly to John Gardner, we discover that the
type of writing that Bellow abandoned is precisely what would
meet Gardner's prescriptions for good fiction. The exuberant,
incontrovertibly *vocal* some might say, Jewish sensibility that
informs the ruminating consciousness of Bellow's post-*Victim*
heroes is, for Gardner and for those critics who feel Bellow to
be more a philosopher than a novelist, at the root of Bellow's
afictionality. For Bellow himself it became the measure of his
fictional freedom.

Part Two_____
Fathers and Sons

Introduction to Part Two

The first two paragraphs of *Dangling Man* (Bellow's first novel) are devoted to an attack on Hemingway and on his code of "hardboileddom." Joseph is sick to death of people who "fly planes, fight bulls or catch tarpon. . . ." (*Dangling Man*, p. 10); he is sick of the way they regard introspective personalities like himself as shameful weaklings. Joseph feels obliged to defend his diary writing and is annoyed that such a defense should be necessary. He won't strangle his emotions, he tells us, he's going to blab, and his blabbing will eventually lead him down paths of seriousness that are closed to the "hardboiled."

Joseph never does give us the unrestricted, emotion-packed inner life that his opening salvo promises, but, ever since Joseph's outburst, Bellow's heroes have been wrestling with the stigma that attaches itself to their anti-Hemingway philosophies. Indeed, we normally think of Norman Mailer as Hemingway's literary progeny, but in terms of Oedipal conflict it is Bellow who is busy with Papa more than the two-fisted author of *The Naked and the Dead.*

Do Bellow's novels really advertise and present "feelings" and the expression of feelings as the supernal elements in human life? Well, yes and no. Bellow certainly seems to want to affirm the value of "feelings"; his heroes derive their positive conceptions of the world from their sentiments rather than from their experience (which is uniformly crisis-filled); and they are constantly reassuring both themselves and the reader that truth comes more often from the heart than the head. However, the fear that "feelings" may indeed be all the things that a dominating male American sensibility says they are seems to haunt both Bellow's heroes and their creator.

At the root of this fear lies the deep suspicion, enunciated by some of the heroes and reinforced by the novels as a whole, that to be inordinately governed by feeling is to risk emasculation. "What was he hanging around for?" Herzog asks, "To follow this career of *personal* relationships until his strength at last gave out? Only to be a smashing success in the private realm. Amorous Herzog seeking love. . . . But this is a female pursuit. This hugging and heartbreak is for women. The occupation of a man is in duty, in use, in civility, in politics in the Aristotelean sense" (*Herzog,* p. 94).

Often we are told that the "feelings" of Bellow's heroes have derived from their soft or oversensitive mothers: Tommy Wilhelm the hero of *Seize The Day* gets "sensitive feelings, a soft heart [and] a brooding nature" (*Seize The Day,* p. 25) from his mother, while Augie March tells us that "where love was concerned I was on my mother's side against the [hard-hearted] Grandma Lausches, Mrs. Renlings and Lucy Magnuses" (*The Adventures of Augie March,* p. 401).

Bellow's exclusively male heroes predominantly assert what Herzog calls the "law of the heart" (*Herzog,* p. 119). However, the fact that such law is, through the terms of their own and Bellow's associations, "feminine" seems to be at the base of much of the heroes' ambivalence about their own selves and about the world. Bellow's heroes love and fear the feminine parts of themselves and half of the time Bellow seems to share rather than deny the vulgarized version of Hemingway, now a cliché of American life, in which poets, writers, and sensitive people in general are considered to be actually "women." Bellow seems unsure whether this is acceptable or a disaster, whether it rewards the sensitive man with additional insight or emasculates him—and probably, according to Bellow, it does both.

Critics have often complained that there are no real women in Bellow's novels[1] and certainly Bellow's imagination does not range very far where his female characters are concerned. But it should not be supposed that Bellow's shadowy women characters remove the possibility of serious engagement with what Bellow conceives of as "the feminine." Bellow's "real women" are firmly settled inside his "real men." They are, in fact, "internal mothers." "External" women in Bellow's canon who are not mothers, that is, wives, girlfriends, and acquaintances, tend to represent limitation and constriction in much the same way as many of the male characters that Bellow's heroes come into contact with. But the "female" inside Bellow's heroes, like the child in them, seems to represent elements in the heroes' being—their "feelings," their "love," their "naiveté"—

that give them pleasure and offer them insight into the true and beneficent nature of the world they inhabit.

However, the more optimistic presentiments and affirmations that the Bellow hero derives from his "internal mother" are almost always undercut. For, each hero in turn is in some manner discomforted by the notion that a failure to acknowledge the harsh realities of life is concomitant with a failure to be a man. Sceptical about the perceptions and assertions that issue from feminine wellsprings—the enlightenment that comes from the deep heart's core—Bellow's heroes rarely have the courage of their convictions.

The threat to the male self is at its greatest when the hero has both the heart of an irrational softy and the head of a bona fide, if eccentric, American intellectual. In the novels that feature such heroes—*Herzog, Mr. Sammler's Planet, Humboldt's Gift*, and, less obviously, *The Adventures of Augie March*—Bellow compensates his protagonists by reasserting, even if ironically, their essential tough-guy natures. Bellow's most sophisticated thinker/feelers love to hang out with underworld types, have a tendency to flirt with criminal behavior themselves, and often wind up in some kind of ambivalent relationship with a criminal whom they detest morally and yet find aesthetically compelling—Augie and Joe Gorman, Sammler and the black pickpocket, Citrine and Cantabile come immediately to mind.

Moses Herzog, in particular, takes great pleasure in acting the tough guy. His girlfriend, Ramona, finds this aspect of his personality one of the funniest things about him.

> "It's the way you try to sound rough and reckless, though—like a guy from Chicago—that's even more amusing."
> "Why amusing?"
> "It's an act. Swagger. It's not really you." (*Herzog*, p. 183)

The "real" Herzog is full of "feelings." But his act seems to be a way of denying them.

Those heroes who do not put on a tough-guy act or become associated with criminals are often compensated for their inner softy-ness by their indisputably masculine size. Asa Leventhal is "large and burly" (*The Victim*, p. 13), Tommy Wilhelm is compared to a hippopotamus and a bear (*Seize The Day*, p. 15), while

Eugene Henderson is a positively gargantuan "six feet four inches tall. Two hundred and thirty pounds" (*Henderson the Rain King*, p. 4).

Ambivalence presides over the presentation of Bellow's heroes but, throughout his canon, two dominant, dialectically opposed chains of association are discernible. At some point in their novels Bellow's heroes will always link themselves or be linked, symbolically or discursively, to children, women, or the feebleminded. These associations are another way of saying that the hero is a "feeling," sensitive person. Thus to grow up, or to be a "man," or to think "rationally" is, Bellow's seems to suggest, to risk sacrificing all feeling, all love, all tenderness, and in some mysterious way all knowledge of the truth. By contrast, Bellow's heroes' adversaries, whether young or old, male or female, are associated with the adult, male world, another way of saying that they are coldhearted. To be an "adult" in Bellow's world is to control your own fate but has little else to commend it.

The Adventures of Augie March and *Seize the Day* are the two novels that reveal most overtly both the ambivalence of Bellow's heroes toward their own "feeling" selves, and Bellow's own ambivalence about what it means to be an adult male in American society. In a fascinating way the ever-present dialectical oppositions of Bellow's canon are, in these novels, hung on a set of Oedipal struggles. In both *Augie* and *Seize the Day,* fathers or parent figures clearly represent limitation, hardheartedness (they are "against love"), the "adult" world, and the business world. Sons, on the other hand, strive for "freedom," are on the side of love (although Augie March ultimately comes to regard it as yet another form of limitation) and feeling, seem to be eternal children, and lack any kind of capacity to deal effectively with the money world.

The world of the "son" is the one that Bellow always seems to want to affirm. But this world is also the world of the internal "child" and "woman" and while Bellow's son-heroes are sympathetically portrayed, we should be aware that what is endearing in their personalities also undercuts their potential to achieve true "manliness."

The world of the "fathers" is, of course, less sympathetically portrayed (Augie March has "Oedipal" struggles with several mother figures, but unlike his own mother they are hardhearted women who in their personalities and in their behavior

belong to the world of the fathers), but these materialistic, authoritarian adults do have a good side. Often they are around
to bail the hero out when he is in trouble and sometimes they
seem legitimately fed up with their "naive" and "childish"
charges. Naturally, to balance things out, Bellow provides an
antidote to their "manliness." In *Augie March* one father figure,
William Einhorn, is paralyzed to such an extent that he can only
move his head and hands, and one of the mother/fathers,
Grandma Lausch, becomes senile. In *Seize the Day,* Tommy
Wilhelm's "adult," realistic father is given one of the ugliest
personalities of any Bellow character.

The Adventures of Augie March and *Seize The Day* are, however,
two of the most illuminating and successful novels in Bellow's
canon. The direct and explicit staging of dialectical conflicts in
Oedipal terms both clarifies and explains Bellow's and his
heroes "ambivalence." In Bellow's first two novels there is no
firm authorial affirmation of the central characters. Here, we
begin to understand how Bellow feels about his child/man
woman/man foolish/wise heroes and just why they are "paralyzed." The "dialectic" is still "static"—Augie and Tommy can
neither "grow up" nor be satisfied with who they are, but its
terms are clear and sharp. Ultimately, on the one side is the big
daddy of business America and on the other is the "childlike"
world of the soul.

The Adventures of Augie March

The Adventures of Augie March is Bellow's tour de force. "The great pleasure of the book," Bellow has written "was that it came easily." All he had to do was "be there with buckets to catch it."[1] For the reader too there is great pleasure to be found in the novel's five hundred pages of energetic first-person narration. Upward of eighty characters are introduced; the action shifts from Chicago to Mexico and on to Paris and Rome; the historical span is equally broad, taking us through three decades from the early 1920s to the immediate postwar period. Best of all, the novel's eponymous hero is larky, bright, mercurial, and aware and, unlike his predecessors, the world that he seeks to affirm is variegated and spacious.

What happened? Bellow tells us that when he began to write *Augie* he felt a spurt of confidence. For some reason "the incredible effrontery of announcing [him]self to the world (. . . the WASP world) as a writer and an artist"[2] ceased to trouble him. As his social inhibitions fell away, his prose too began to loosen up. *Augie* features catalogues; enumerations; high-flown intellectual references radically coupled with street jargon; deep breaths of sentences, most of which are spoken in the engaging, ingenuous voice of a picaresque hero.

Much of Bellow's own enthusiasm and exuberance has been passed on to the critics. "The variety of language and the range of allusions are very like the variety and range of Melville's *Moby Dick*," Allen Guttman has written. For Robert Shulman, *Augie* reveals Bellow as belonging to "a line of descent (and dissent) characterized by the intellectual comedy and expansive prose of writers like Burton, Sterne and Joyce." Richard Chase has invoked in comparison Rabelais, Whitman, Melville, [and] Joyce. "In *Augie March*," says Eusebio Rodrigues "Bellow reached back to the . . . open-ended forms of American fiction used by Melville and Mark Twain." While, most recently, Malcolm Bradbury has pointed to the novel's conveyed sense of "Dickensian abundance."[3]

Writing *Augie,* Bellow discovered that he could explore his chosen themes without necessarily confining himself to a miserable hero and a claustrophobic environment. The social impotence of Joseph in *Dangling Man* is transformed into Augie's celebration of his apparently unwilled free spin over the surface of the earth. Similarly, Asa Leventhal's paranoia *(The Victim),* turned on its head, becomes Augie's sense of wonder. There can be no doubt that *Augie March* represents a grand departure from Bellow's first two novels.[4]

However, while Bellow may have liberated himself and freed his prose style, he did not go so far as to free the hero of his novel from what were rapidly becoming definitive Bellovian dilemmas.

The central focus of *Augie March* is on the struggle of its hero to secure what he calls "an independent fate" (p. 401). This struggle is hampered by the fact that Augie compulsively searches out relationships with characters who are, in the manner of an authoritarian parent, likely to want to limit, form, and control him. Consequently, the situations that Augie gets himself into rarely square with his notions of what constitutes independence.

Augie's main conflict, as he is usually half-aware, is with himself. Desiring, like Joseph and Leventhal, to be free of familial influence, Augie simultaneously desires to be the beloved member of a sympathetic family. Displaying a propensity to constant travel that seems to be an expression of his freedom, Augie yearns to curtail his movements and settle down. Wishing to remain "independent," Augie is desperate for love, which he regards as fundamentally imprisoning. Symbolically demonstrating his "freedom" by committing petty crimes, Augie nevertheless respects the main body of the law. "I can't take [the] very things I want" (p. 514), says Augie, but this is largely because the things that he wants are mutually exclusive. On the face of it, Augie, unlike Joseph and Leventhal, is an avoider of limits but, on a deeper level, he is as much a "dangling man" as his two predecessors.

Augie's internal conflicts are expressed and externalized in a series of relationships that involve him with surrogate parents. Augie is the "by-blow of a traveling man" (p. 125) and the son of a weak self-effacing mother, so his own parents exert almost no influence upon him. Instead, throughout the novel, the rhythm of the plot swings Augie alternately between powerful and manipulative mother and father figures: Grandma Lausch, William Einhorn, Mrs. Renling, Simon March, Thea Fenchel, Hymie Basteshaw, Stella Chesney, and Mintouchian. Augie both craves and resists the company of these parent figures (some of whom are actually brothers, lovers, and wives) and his desire to achieve an "independent fate" is, at one level, always synonymous with his desire to break free from the domination of one of what he calls his "destiny moulders" (p. 524).

The Adventures of Augie March is Bellow's attempt to write a *Bildungsroman*. However, *Bildungsromans* demand progress and growth on the part of the hero; a character must get "built" or at least come to the point where his "taking of a first step" is credible, and the development of his personality should be more or less linear. These generic qualities are fundamentally at odds with the kind of characterization in which Bellow specializes. It is Augie's fate to repeat a pattern of experience in which he is controlled rather than controlling. He never *learns* anything from what happens to him and, like all those who do not learn from history whether personal or social, Augie is doomed to repeat it. Throughout the novel, the reader waits for Augie to emerge into adulthood and cast aside his ambivalences—but he never does. For, beneath the dynamic character-filled narrative surface of the novel, Bellow's "static dialectic" has Augie in its grip.

Were Augie to "grow up," one might assume that the conflict between, say, his desire to be independent and his yearning for deep attachment to a mentor—whether brother, wife, or lover—would come close to being resolved, or at least understood. "Kindly explain!" Augie demands at one point in the novel, "An independent fate and love too—what confusion!" (p. 401). But no answer can be provided. For to do so would be to expose the futility of Augie's quest. Bellow cannot allow his hero to conclude that he cannot have his dialectical cake and eat it too. For to do so would be to undermine the "negative energy" that drives both Augie and the novel in which he appears. No matter how many times the hammer of experience hits Augie over the head, he must continue to search both for love and for a pristine autonomous self. Augie's "adventures" have large surface differences, which account for their fascination, but at base they are the same "adventure"—a conflict with adulthood and with all that it symbolizes for Bellow and Augie both.

Grandma Lausch is the first of the "parent figures" to dominate Augie. This autocratic old Russian lady is nominally a lodger at the March family home in Chicago, having been unceremoniously abandoned by her two sons—"The daughters-in-law did not want her" (p. 5). Grandma is quick to replace her lost sons with Augie and his older brother, Simon: and finding that their soft, half-blind mother offers little in the way of opposition, Grandma soon establishes herself as the head of the March household. From this lofty position, Grandma issues orders and gives instructions. She wants Augie and Simon to be gentlemen; they must also know the ways of the world. Coached by Grandma, Augie is easily able to cheat the Welfare Board; but if she encourages this petty crime, Grandma is equally determined to instill into her wards a respect for learning and scholarship. In exchange for her pedagogic services, Grandma merely demands that the March family display a sense of unending gratitude and indebtedness. She dramatizes herself as a suffering altruist and the drama is marvellously comic. Augie feels that "if wit and discontent don't necessarily go together, it wasn't from the old woman that I learned it" (p. 7).

Augie's attitude toward this domineering old lady is highly ambivalent. Listing Grandma's faults at length, Augie is always quick to qualify his criticisms. "Still the old lady had a heart" (p. 10), he interpolates, or "The old *grand-dame* I don't want to be misrepresenting her" (p. 11). Toward the end of her "reign," Grandma commits her cardinal sin and arranges for Augie's imbecile brother, Georgie, to be transported to a home. Grandma's crime is not so much her insistence upon what is perhaps inevitable but the almost sadistic pleasure that she derives from the pain that she causes. Despite his hurt, Augie is still willing to mitigate her offence. "I don't want to make out that her position was all wicked evil. . . ." (p. 51). Augie admires Grandma's resilience and is somewhat in awe of her regal style; yet he is at odds with the absolutist philosophy that governs her actions and is perturbed by her vindictive behavior.

Augie's relationship with Grandma sets the pattern for all of his subsequent relationships with authority figures. He is equally ambivalent about practically all the major influences on his life. For example, Augie finds William Einhorn, his first employer, brave, acute, and endowed with a praiseworthy, "philosophical capacity" (p. 60), and yet on occasion he appears to Augie "selfish, jealous, autocratic, carp-mouth, and hypocritical" (p. 99). Even the murderous Basteshaw, a character with whom Augie is cut adrift in a lifeboat toward the end of the novel, is described as having "some nobility of heart and was a good guy in some mysterious respects" (p. 502).

Augie's ambivalence is partly determined by the contrasting qualities of the characters who surround him, but has deeper roots in his own personality. Augie has a tendency to both elevate and denigrate any one with whom he engages in a "child/ parent" relationship. If Augie were ever to take to the analyst's couch (as Moses Herzog does), one of Bellow's unpleasant shrinks would no doubt home in on his illegitimacy, absent father, and pathetic mother. However, because we are analyzing a Bellow character and not Augie himself, the problem can be seen and explained in more general terms. Like Joseph and Leventhal before him, Augie is never sure who is worthy in his life and who is worthless.

Augie delights in endowing his "destiny moulders" with what Robert Shulman has called "an aura of epic dignity and imperial magnitude."[5] Augie's method of characterization is to recurrently allude to classical, biblical, and historical figures and then compare them to characters in his own life. As John Berryman puts it, these "Overlords" hang over the novel like "the marvellous vast heads of statues in some of Watteau's pictures overlooking his lovers."[6] Grandma Lausch, we are told, is "like a pharaoh or a Caesar" (p. 37) and a modern "Machiavelli" (ibid); similitudes she shares with William Einhorn, who is like "Caesar, Machiavelli [and] Ulysses" (p. 60). The demeanor of Augie's brother Simon reminds Augie of a "sovereign" (p. 216) or "a king" (p. 424). The examples proliferate.

Augie's objective in thus aggrandizing his surrogate parents is ostensibly to indicate how marvellous heroic and aristocratic qualities can just as easily appear among a population of "teeming democrats" (p. 60), "how the traits we honor in . . . fabulous names" are equally present in an Einhorn or Lausch.

However, while Augie delights in uncovering the extraordinary in the ordinary, and revealing a Lausch or Einhorn (whose own name has a nice mythological ring to it) in all their glory, he is also bent on stressing the shoddiness and pettiness of Lausch and Einhorn, the vanity of Mrs. Renling, the coldhearted manipulations of his brother Simon and the vast carelessness of his girlfriend, Thea Fenchel. For all Augie's strenuous aggrandizement of his "parent figures," he is finally bent on revealing the dwarf's heart in the giant's ego.

"Offer him gold and he says, no, he chooses shit" (p. 153), says Mrs. Renling when Augie refuses her offer to legally adopt him and make him Augie Renling. However, by the end of the novel, it is quite clear that all the characters whom Augie has euphorically praised are actually "shit" while Augie himself, who has depicted his own personality in more modest terms, shines out in all his glory. In fact, in *The Adventures of Augie March,* Joseph's and Leventhal's genuine confusion as to who is to be valued and who not seems to have been transformed into Augie's consciously false denigrations of his worthy self and unconvincing elevations of his worthless acquaintances.

From *Augie March* onward in Bellow's canon, the hero will *appear* to be in a dilemma over the true nature of his own character—usually over questions as to whether or not he is child or man, naive or wise, dependent or independent—but (with the exception of *Seize the Day*) the overall effect of the novels is to leave the reader with no such doubts. We know, even if Herzog claims not to, that, child or man, he is "gold" and his adversaries "shit." It is perhaps partly for this reason that Augie and almost all the heroes who come after him can remain such cheerful "dangling men."

On the surface, Augie's ambivalence toward his parent figures seems to correspond to Joseph and Leventhal's equally ambivalent attitudes toward both their families and the environments that they inhabit. Like them, Augie seems obsessed with the idea that he may well be little more than the sum of his influences. As Augie announces early in the novel, "All the influences were lined up waiting for me. I was born and there they were to form me, which is why I tell you more of them than of myself" (p. 43).

However, when it comes down to it, Augie tends to stress his opposition and independence. Again his relationship with Grandma Lausch is paradigmatic. Augie is quick to learn. What he learns, however, is derived less through the pedagogic persistence of the old lady than through his observation of her "style." It is not Grandma's methods of dealing with the world that impress Augie so much as her imperial manner.

Grandma's line is to endeavor to convince Augie and Simon

of the need to be constantly on guard; they are fools, innocents surrounded by "the cunning-hearted and tough . . . a desperate mankind without feelings" (p. 10). Less interested in Grandma's philosophy than in the brilliance of her invective, Augie is entranced by the delights of her linguistic virtuosity, in particular her Yiddish-translated epithet making. Rather than her ideas, it is the range and manner of Grandma's verbal performance that Augie incorporates into his being. Augie's response to Grandma is not moral but aesthetic and can be said to correspond to the kind of delight in words that Stephen Dedalus discovers at school or at his parents' dinner table. The lessons that Grandma unwittingly provides in the imaginative use of language, like those of Stephen's schoolboy friends, are naive but trenchant.

> She called Kotzie, "the baked apple," she called Mrs. Kreindl "the secret goose," Lubin "the shoemaker's son," the dentist "the butcher," the butcher "the timid swindler." (P. 7)

Along with the informal education that Grandma provides with her kitchen wisdom, she also endeavors to open up the gates of knowledge in more orthodox fashion. The first book that we hear of Augie devouring is an 1892 edition of the *Encyclopedia Americana,* a gift from Grandma.

Once again a pattern is set in which Augie indirectly learns from his "benefactors." Reading Simon's copy of the *Iliad* Augie is at once enchanted by the story of Achilles and Briseis and yet drawn to listen in on a conversation taking place in the same room. The subject of the conversation, fascinating for a young boy, is money and women (p. 26). From Einhorn Augie receives a charred set of the *Harvard Classics,* rescued from a fire Einhorn has set on his premises. The "fixed" knowledge contained therein perfectly complements Einhorn's floating erudition.

In the early stages of Augie's "adventures," what he learns from his observation of the charismatic figures who surround him is always supplemented by a bibliography. Later in the novel, when Augie begins stealing books in partnership with his Mexican friend, Padilla, he becomes loath to part with the stolen goods and prefers to read them himself.

The Adventures of Augie March is the closest that Bellow has ever come to writing a portrait of the artist as a young man.

But, Bellow's young man does not go on to be an artist. Instead, his "artistic" education, informal, broad, orthodox, and experimental, becomes the measure and mirror of his personality. Augie, we understand, both wishes to conform and yearns to be unfettered. In terms of substance, however, his wonderfully open, distinctively American education only prepares him for a life of petty crime. At the end of his novel he does not go off to Rome to write *The Adventures of Augie March* but merely to jot down some memoirs and rest up from his latest round of postwar black-market swindles.

As Grandma ages, her authority over the March family begins to wane and, after she has suffered a particularly nasty fall (symbolically enough on an election day), it becomes virtually extinct. As far as Augie's behavior is concerned, her influence has, in any case, always been rather less than she imagined it to be. By the age of twelve, Augie tells us, Grandma felt that "she had already formed me" (p. 24), but the reader is aware of her self-delusion, for unbeknownst to Grandma, Augie has for some time been running with a classmate—Jimmy Klein. Klein specializes in petty swindles and Augie is his willing accomplice. Thus it is not so much Augie's active opposition to Grandma's attempts to form him that reduce her power as his susceptibility to other influences. Augie is easy prey for anyone who has a strong sense of what he wants and a propensity to direct the lives of others.

Klein's influence increases as Grandma Lausch's diminishes, and a pattern is established that is to last throughout the novel. After the brief period of Grandma Lausch's absolute control, Augie is practically always under the simultaneous "instruction" of both authoritarian "parent figures" and, somewhat less influential laissez-faire criminals. He swings wildly between the two sets of characters, neither wholly embracing, nor wholly rejecting the "philosophies" that they espouse.

While still a high school junior, Augie begins to work for William Einhorn, whom he describes as "the first superior man I knew" (p. 60). Einhorn is a cripple, confined to a wheelchair and totally paralyzed apart from his hands and head. Einhorn's attitude to Augie is homiletic and avuncular, but, although he denies it, Augie tends to adopt something of a filial attitude towards his employer. Throughout the novel, in fact, Augie seems to deny the parent/child relationships he sets up by metaphorically casting them as those of uncle or aunt to nephew. For

example, Augie feels that for Mrs. Renling he is "something of
a nephew" (p. 132), and while in the company of Mr. Renling,
he has a sense of himself as a "gilded nephew" (p. 133). In
Augie's opinion his advice-giving friend Clem Tambow also
speaks to him like "an uncle to a nephew" (p. 203). Augie's need
to thus displace himself is yet another manifestation of his ambivalence toward those who seek to control him. He will be a
"son" only on his own terms.

Interestingly, Bellow's novels are full of uncles, nieces, and
nephews (we might think of Artur Sammler who lives with his
niece, Margotte, rather than with his daughter, Shula, or the
childless Albert Corde locked in an Oedipal struggle with his
dreadful nephew, Morton Zaehner), but direct parent/child relationships and confrontations are much less common. It is
hard to know what is at the root of Bellow's distaste for novels
featuring the nuclear family—perhaps the imagination has
freer range when distant relatives are brought together?

Certainly, William Einhorn (a kind of honorable uncle) is one
of Bellow's most vivid portraits. Riding Augie's back into a
whorehouse, cheating gangsters in shady business deals, edit-
ing *The Shut In,* a magazine for cripples, or freely quoting from
Plutarch, the Bible, and Shakespeare, Einhorn, despite his
enormous handicap, is as various in his employment and wide
ranging in his metaphoric associations as Augie himself.

Augie becomes Einhorn's "arms and legs" (p. 61) and, as a
result, something of a captive audience for his employer.

> Einhorn had a teaching turn similar to Grandma Lausch's,
> both believed they could show you what could be done with
> the world, where it gave or resisted, where you could be
> confident and run or where you could only feel your way and
> were forced to blunder. (P. 67)

As in the case of Grandma Lausch, however, Augie tends to
disregard Einhorn's messages, and continues to insist that he is
not "really his disciple" (p. 60).

In identical fashion to his experiences with Grandma Lausch,
Augie comes under the influence of a criminal—Joe Gorman—
just as Einhorn's hold on him is beginning to slip. Almost completely ruined by the Crash of 1929, Einhorn has neither the
means nor the reason to continue to employ Augie. Hanging
around the poolroom that is the last vestige of Einhorn's prop-

erty empire, Augie comes into contact with Gorman. Gorman is "very bright, handsome and slim" (p. 114), and Augie's decision to take part in the robbery of a leather-goods shop (which turns out disastrously) seems determined less by his material needs than by his desire to experience the *frisson* of a crime. In fact, despite Augie's constant reminders to the reader that he lacks the true sense of being a criminal, he is repeatedly drawn to commit petty crimes. In the course of the novel he swindles a large store, burgles a shop, gets involved in illegal immigrant running, steals books, and works the postwar black market in army surplus goods.

Augie's attraction to crime seems partly derived from the sense of freedom that accompanies the acts of an "outlaw." However, to see Augie within the tradition of Romantic criminals is to miss the point that his boundary breaking is only halfhearted. Like Bellow's other Chicago types, Moses Herzog and Charlie Citrine, Augie is drawn to a mode of life that he is morally in conflict with. However, like Artur Sammler, the aging Polish-Jewish hero of *Mr. Sammler's Planet,* Augie also seems to be aesthetically attracted to criminals. Augie finds in Joe Gorman a similar kind of "princeliness" in appearance and style to that which Sammler discovers in the criminal with whom he is associated—the black pickpocket.

However, the freedom of action that a crime offers and the terrible beauty of its commission are not enough to wholly draw Augie into the orbit of hard-core criminals. For the greater part of the novel, Augie remains uneasy about his occasional forays outside the law. He knows he is on the wrong track but is hard put to establish in his mind what are the right tracks. Only toward the end of the novel, when Augie's vision of "the axial lines of life with respect to which you must be straight" (p. 454) finally takes concrete form, do we realize the immense contradiction between his desires and his behavior. In that formulation of his vision, what Augie wants to achieve is "truth, love, peace, bounty, usefulness, harmony!" (p. 454). In conversation with his friend Clem Tambow, he outlines the plan that he has in mind.

I aim to get myself a piece of property and settle down on it . . . what I'd like most is to get married and set up a kind of home and teach school. . . . I'd get my mother out of the blind home and my brother George up from the South. . . . (P. 456)

Augie's dream never materializes. His desire to be a former rather than one of the formed is more than outweighed by his deep fear that domestic life is a form of paralysis and by his equally deep resistances to taking on "adult" responsibilities. Paradoxically, the "free" life that Augie appears to opt for contains enough paralyzing episodes to last him several lifetimes.

Even Augie's criminal acquaintances and accomplices turn out, in their own way, to be "parent figures," directing and arranging Augie's life for him. It is Augie's misfortune to be a character about whom "something . . . suggest[s] adoption" and it is his greater misfortunate to be constantly running into characters who are "especially adoption minded" (p. 151). More than any other Bellow hero, Augie's behavior corresponds to Joseph's chilling assessment of man's relation to his own freedom—that "we are afraid to govern ourselves" and yearn to "run out . . . choose a master, roll over on our backs and ask for the leash" (*Dangling Man,* pp. 167–68). One of the reasons that *The Adventures of Augie March* gives the illusion of "freedom" is because its hero is ebullient, but Augie's cheerfulness is hardly earned.

Indeed, telling us more of his "influences" than of himself and defined more accurately by submission than "opposition," Augie sometimes runs the risk of disappearing altogether from his own narrative. Moreover, Bellow seems to go out of his way to symbolically stress Augie's "not thereness." For example, throughout the novel, Augie happily submits to the sartorial whims of whoever's control he happens to be under: Mrs. Renling makes "a clotheshorse" (p. 130) of him; brother Simon flings his silk shirts on the floor for Augie to pick up and keep; while Thea Fenchel lavishly outfits Augie in the *à la mode* outfits of a contemporary huntsman. When Augie is not being dressed by someone else, he is usually to be found sporting the uniform of an employment or of a service.

Late in the novel it is no surprise to find Augie contemplating, with a mixture of loathing and delight, Thea Fenchel's pet snakes as they cast their skins—for, the identity is a strong one.

Toughest of all was the casting of skins, which was like labor when they couldn't writhe out of the epidermis. . . . But then they would gleam out one day and their freshness and jewellery would give me even more pleasure, their enemy, and I would like to look at the cast skin from which they were regenerated. (P. 369)

Each new set of clothes that Augie acquires, and each new identity, gives him pleasure, like the snakes' skins, only at the initial moment of transformation. Subsequently Augie spends long periods of time writhing out of his own epidermis.

Of all Bellow's heroes, Augie is the only one to have had his "not-thereness" unanimously identified by the critics. At the time of the novel's publication, Robert Penn Warren wrote that "it is hard to give substance to a man who has no commitments," and his sentiment has been widely endorsed. Tony Tanner, for example, finds Augie to be "rather light, somewhat blurred and insubstantial, a diffuse presence rather than an individual person."[7]

Augie's "not-thereness" is extreme. For this reason it is tempting to momentarily put aside considerations of Bellow's idiosyncratic modes of characterization and attempt, instead, to interpret Augie's character in broader terms. For, the publication of *The Adventures of Augie March* coincided in the United States with that of Ralph Ellison's *Invisible Man* and in Germany with Thomas Mann's *Confessions of Felix Krull, Confidence Man* and, collectively, the three novels consolidate a picture of a new, socially disenfranchised postwar hero. Moreover, the first-person narratives of the three writers' identity-less heroes are all pyrotechnic displays of language or of the imagination and seem to derive their fire and light from the displaced energy of their socially impotent narrators. Augie thus suffers the double liability of being both a representative "invisible man" of the times and a characteristically disembodied Bellovian hero.

The particularities of Augie's philosophical and existential dilemmas are, however, pure Bellow. Suspicious of order and limit, Augie remains threatened by disorder and "freedom." He is thus faced with the problem that all Bellow's heroes share of how to break free without breaking loose. On the surface, attempting to secure "freedom," Augie constantly reveals himself as more conservatively attempting to establish a set of limits for himself within which he can experience a measure of freedom. One brief dramatic episode involving Augie in a criminal caper with Joe Gorman both literally and symbolically conveys the extent of Augie's problems.

Gorman employs Augie as a driver to run illegal immigrants across the Canadian border and into the States. On their way north, while the plan is still being set up, Gorman and Augie run afoul of the police. Unbeknownst to Augie, he has been driving a stolen car. The cops pull them over at a wayside gas station. Gorman draws a gun (another special effect of which Augie has been unaware) and Augie decides to make a run for it. He escapes and makes it to the nearby township of Lackawanna (placenames are not usually heavily symbolic in Bellow's novels—but this one is).

The crime that Augie was about to commit—illegally crossing borders—and his inability to go through with it accurately convey important contradictory elements in Augie's personality: both his desire to be "free" and his simultaneous fear of the danger that it entails.

Augie's dual allegiances to "freedom" and to limitation dictate the subrhythm of his behavior. For, while there is always a big daddy or big mummy in the background of his life, their influence is always at its greatest when Augie is on the rebound from a chastening experience with one of his criminal friends.

Most frequently Augie is bailed out by his brother Simon. Simon March is a peripatetic figure in the novel, appearing throughout as a kind of amalgamation of many of the forces that Augie both submits to and resists. Something of a bully, Simon considers Augie too "hasty, too enthusiastic . . . a *schlemiel*" (p. 194). In his hard-nosed attitude to business and his authoritative and patronizing treatment of his family and friends, Simon is recognizably a member of that group of older brothers in Bellow's novels whom the hero loves despite himself. The attitude of Amos to Joseph in *Dangling Man,* Will and Shura to Moses Herzog in *Herzog,* or of Julius to Charlie Citrine in *Humboldt's Gift,* is almost identical to Simon's attitude to Augie. In every case the hero is glad to accept money and cast-off clothing from his brother, and while in his company is happy to act out the role of sentimental, worldly innocent that the brother prescribes for him.

Augie moves in and out of Simon's sphere of influence. Apparently desperate for familial love, Augie is moved that Simon thinks of him even when Simon's thoughts are merely to incorporate Augie in his own grand and Machiavellian designs. Simon's particular plan for Augie involves marriage to Lucy Magnus, a rich girl who is the cousin of Simon's own wealthy fiancé Charlotte Magnus. Unashamedly, Simon's quest is for money and power. As Augie believes himself to be a searcher after love, the two brothers often find themselves at odds. Sometimes Simon's behavior is so callous that Augie cannot help but detest him, yet his animosity is always softened by the sudden and surprising bursts of fraternal affection that Augie feels.

Scornful, manipulative, and sometimes brutal, Simon is the most effective of those figures who try to shape Augie's life. In Simon's presence Augie seems doubly impotent and powerfully drawn to give himself up to Simon's schemes. Believing that he will be rewarded with "love," Augie is willing to sacrifice almost anything; and most certainly, his identity. All Bellow heroes who have elder siblings yearn to be loved by them. However, the type of love that they demand is only granted at the expense of their own self-effacement. But, this seems to be precisely what the heroes want—to remain children in the eyes of their brothers and sisters. Potentially, the love of a sibling is adequate compensation for the hero's other troubles. Toward the end of the novel Augie tells us

> I love my brother very much. I never meet him again without the utmost love filling me up. He has it too, though we both seem to fight it. (P. 533)

From the reader's point of view, however, Augie appears sadly deluded. As in *Humboldt's Gift,* the older brother is hardly revealed in the novel as sharing in the passion of the younger. Simon becomes yet another character whose philosophy is anathema to Augie, whose behavior often disgusts him and whom Augie is unable entirely to repudiate.

One of the most disturbing features of *The Adventures of Augie March* is that "growing up" is imaged as bringing along with it no special increase of control over one's own fate. At the precise midpoint of the novel, after Augie has concluded his "adventures" with Grandma Lausch, Einhorn, and The Renlings and after he has had a particularly nasty set-to with Simon, Augie announces

> I was no child now, neither in age nor in protectedness, and I was thrown for fair on the free spinning of the world. (P. 285)

However, if at this point, both Augie and the reader expect something to change in the nature of Augie's relationships, they are wrong. Bellow never follows up on Augie's dramatic assertion of his own independence. Augie actually remains a child "in protectedness" (for which read emotional and

financial dependence) until the very end of the novel, falling in
first with the schemes of Thea Fenchel and finally with those of
Stella Chesney and Mintouchian. *The Adventures of Augie March*
has often been compared to *The Adventures of Huckleberry Finn,*
mostly in terms of the two novels' picaresque form;[8] it is perhaps worth noting that Augie is well into his thirties at the
conclusion of his novel, while Huck remains a child throughout, the novel ending when Huck lights out for the territories
(and adulthood?) at the tender age of fourteen.

In the second half of *Augie March,* Bellow runs out of steam.
The characterizations are less sharp and when Augie leaves
Chicago (as he does almost immediately), the marvellously
evocative descriptions of urban life give way to a tamer, more
predictable and more highly conventionalized account of exotic
Mexico. Grandma Lausch and Einhorn are among Bellow's
finest imaginative creations, beside whom Thea Fenchel, Basteshaw, Stella, and Mintouchian seem poor shadows. It is the
Chicago personalities that engage Bellow and it is the city and
its immediate environs that seem to encourage his Dreiserian
attention to detail.

In Mexico, however, because the characters who surround
him are a little more shadowy, Augie himself begins to come
into his own. And it is while staying in Thea Fenchel's ironically
named Casa Descuitada (Carefree House) that Augie comes
closest to understanding the true nature of his quest for an
"independent fate."

Augie is in Mexico, ostensibly, to hunt giant iguanas with a
tamed, trained eagle. The hunt, naturally, is not his idea but
Thea's. Thea is "one of those people who are so certain of their
convictions that they can fight for them in the body" (p. 316).
The usual ambivalence that Augie feels toward such domineering personalities is, in Thea's case, tempered by the fact that
Augie is in love with her. Thea's accouterments: guns, Leicas,
boots, cars, and most important of all, large amounts of money
that she treats with aristocratic carelessness, give her an erotic
edge that additionally unbalances Augie.

As a result, Augie's love affair with Thea tests one of his most
treasured principles, and brings into conflict the two most vital
and opposing areas of his being. For, the desire to love and be
loved contradicts at the deepest level Augie's yearning to discover his holy grail of an "independent fate."

While their affair is in its infancy, Augie is willing to set aside his deepest fears, overcome, as he is, with ardor and passion.

> Say if the main bonds of attachment are death ropes, crazy, in the end, at least I felt them now as connexions of joy, and if that were a deception it would never appear more substantial or marvellous. . . . (P. 322)

Yet as soon as the relationship begins to lose its early bloom, the "connexions of joy" do indeed metamorphose into "death ropes." For Augie, as for all Bellow's heroes, deep attachment, after a brief fireworks display, is deathly. It is hardly a life-affirming view of adult life. However, it is a not uncommon view of the way things are. More significantly, Augie's relationship with Thea almost forces him to "grow up" and recognize the mutual exclusiveness of his twin desires for love and independence. However, Bellow cannot allow Augie to resolve his problems by understanding them. For, Augie's problems and his search for their solution are the raison d'etre of the novel.

Predictably, if we have been following the pattern of Augie's behavior, his adventures in Mexico end in disaster. The eagle, called "Caligula," refuses to live up to its name and will not fulfill the role that has been assigned to it by nature. Perversely, Caligula declines to have any part in lizard snatching. With Augie and Thea in Mexico, Bellow has a good time parodying Hemingway's huntsmen. Moreover he manages to sneak a historical footnote into the novel when Trotsky puts in an appearance in the village where Augie is staying. But the whole extended episode, which culminates in Augie's breakup with Thea and meeting with wife-to-be, Stella Chesney, engages us with little more than the plot.

In the final stages of Augie's "adventures," we find Augie enlisted into the navy and packed off to fight the Nazis. As luck would have it Augie's ship is torpedoed before it has fired a shot in anger and Augie is cast adrift in a lifeboat with a murderous lunatic—Basteshaw. Tying up Augie in the boat, Basteshaw literally enacts what has been Augie's metaphoric fate throughout. A paralyzed captive, Augie is obliged to listen to Basteshaw's fanatical and absolutist ravings until he finally manages to free himself. The episode is profound in its symbolization, for it seems to have reverberations throughout Bel-

low's canon. In order to free himself, Augie must work up a
physical energy that seems to figuratively correspond to all the
intellectual energy that Bellow's late heroes produce to counteract their own "paralyses." Hymie Basteshaw is the most extreme of Bellow's authoritarian, know-all figures, but his relationship vis-à-vis Augie is the ur-relationship of Bellow's fiction.
All Bellow's heroes have to be "tied up" before they can get
their juices flowing and discover the range and extent of their
powers.

At the novel's conclusion we find Augie married to the attractive, untrustworthy Stella Chesney, a character whom Bellow
never fully develops. Augie as a husband is, however, no less
desperate in his need for a "mentor." The last of his "influences" is his wife's friend, Mintouchian, an Armenian businessman. Something of a guru, the charismatic Mintouchian
carries around with him an aura of wisdom and secrecy. What
he has to say, however, is not substantially of any more interest
to Augie than was Grandma Lausch's kitchen wisdom. From
Augie's point of view, the only vital element in their relationship is his "requirement" that Mintouchian behave paternalis-
tically and act authoritatively. Mintouchian obliges by taking
Augie into his employ.

Tying together in his personality both the philosophical and
criminal strands of Augie's "influences," Mintouchian attempts
to both educate Augie and involve him in shady business dealings on the black market. At the end of the novel we thus find
Augie still to be a kind of intellectual and criminal apprentice.
In order to complete the circle of Augie's last adventure, it only
remains for Bellow to disappoint him in love: and this he duly
does when Mintouchian, in a quasi-subtle way informs Augie
that his wife has been keeping secrets from him.

The Adventures of Augie March begins with a bang and while it
does not exactly end in a whimper, the early promise of an
unfettered style and open-ended experience is never fulfilled.
The famous opening sentence of the novel is deceiving.

I am an American Chicago born—Chicago, that somber
city—and go at things as I have taught myself, free-style, and
will make the record in my own way: first to knock, first
admitted; sometimes an innocent knock, sometimes a not so
innocent. (P. 3)

For, as we know from Bellow's comments on Joyce, he is not a novelist who likes the "power of the mind" to be "nullified" by the "volume of experience."[9] Augie's democratic promise to himself to make the record in his own way, "free-style," does not take account of his puppet master. Bellow stringently patterns Augie's experiences. While Augie is apparently involved in a wide range of activities and "adventures," the essential structure of his behavior and thought remains the same. Thus the "experience" that Augie is required to order is always neatly packaged to fit the dialectical categories of both his and Bellow's mind.

Similarly, the characters who populate *Augie March* appear to be drawn from Bellow's open response to a pluralistic world. However, as the novel progresses, Bellow's modes of characterization narrow down Augie's world to one in which a character can only take shape as a former or one of the formed. Einhorn's classification of human beings into those who "screwed or were screwed . . . did the manipulating or were roughly handled, tugged and bobbed by their fates" (p. 73) is, as Tony Tanner has suggested, a valid mode of distinguishing the characters of *Augie March*.[10]

Nevertheless, *Augie March* is a great book. As Albert J. Guerard has written, "it is impossible not to recognize the magnitude and seriousness of its aim."[11] Within that seriousness, especially in the first half of the book, is humor, vivid portraiture, and Bellow at the height of his descriptive powers evoking the smells, sights, and sounds of Chicago. Evoking them as if they had come into his blood with his first breaths—as if, in fact, he and not Augie was the American, Chicago born, rather than a child of Lachine, Quebec.

5_____

Seize the Day

Seize the Day is Bellow's most tightly constructed work. The novella is divided into seven chapters that bring us from morning to late afternoon on its hero, Tommy Wilhelm's, "day of reckoning" (p. 97). It is also neatly divided in two. The first half is dominated by Wilhelm's relationship with his authoritarian, intractable father, Dr. Adler, and the second by his dealings with a manipulative and mercurial "surrogate father," Dr. Tamkin. Tamkin's first appearance comes at precisely the midpoint of the novella, and, like Cordelia and The Fool, the two doctors never appear on stage together.

The central issue of *Seize the Day* is an examination of the relative merits of "feelings" and "rationality" as tools for interpreting the world. The ideational positions of the novella's three main characters seem almost as neatly arranged as Bellow's chapters. Wilhelm and Tamkin largely represent "feelings," while Adler comes out of the "rationality" corner. What the novella most profoundly reveals, however, is just how central "ambivalence" is to Bellow's modes of characterization and in what ways the ambivalent presentation of character reports the fundamental concerns of Bellow's fiction.

Wilhelm's personality is governed by two sets of beliefs, which, appropriately enough, are often aligned with the term *Romantic*. On the one hand, he tends to live off his sensibilities, and on the other, he is ruled by the idea that suffering is part of "the business of life" (p. 56).

When we are first introduced to Wilhelm it is the suffering part of him that is in ascendance. Out of work and separated from his wife, who is demanding increased support payments, Wilhelm is in a financial bind. Wilhelm hopes that his wealthy father will bail him out and to expedite matters he has taken a room in the Upper West Side hotel where Dr. Adler is a resident. However, no parental aid is forthcoming. Moreover the

96

eighty-year-old Adler is quite disgusted with the pathetic dependency of his forty-four-year-old son.

Wilhelm is full of self-pity and self-indulgence. He both loathes and loves himself and his self-absorption is hardly sympathetic. More than any other Bellow hero, Wilhelm's sense of self is dependent upon his maintaining a state of crisis in his life.

> If he didn't keep his troubles before him he risked losing them altogether and he knew by experience that this was worse. (P. 43)

This internal affirmation of sickness is externally identifiable through the role of "patient" that Wilhelm submits to in his relationships both with his father and with Tamkin. Of Adler we learn that "he behaved towards his son as he had formerly done towards his patients" (p. 11), while Tamkin, who claims to be a psychologist but is clearly a quack, tells Wilhelm that he has been "treating" (p. 73) him for some time without his knowing it.

From the first pages of the novella it is clear that Bellow has decided to concentrate his attention on a hero for whom it is difficult to feel pity and whose personality is hardly engaging.[1] As we witness Wilhelm cranking himself up to ask Dad for a loan, we are given to understand that he is a character who is both unwilling to take responsibility for his own actions and too quick to demand cover from others for his own mistakes.

Wilhelm is, then, essentially revealed to the reader as an overgrown child. Nevertheless, Bellow has also cast him as the representative of ideas that appear worthy and humane and, while elements of Wilhelm's bloated "Romantic" self remain objects of criticism, the fact that he gives precedence to "feelings" (an inheritance from his mother) (p. 25) as a governing principles in his life seems designed to redeem him in the reader's eyes.

In stark contrast to Wilhelm, old Dr. Adler is presented as a ruthless, hard-nosed realist who berates and batters his son, accusing him of irrationality. However, as the novel progresses it becomes clear that many of Adler's criticisms of his son are, to some extent justified. The adolescent Wilhelm, who would blame anybody but himself for his own ills, does make what appear to be tiresomely exorbitant demands on his father. Ad-

ler remains meanspirited and selfish but nevertheless receives
some small measure of justification for his actions.

The ambivalence that presides over the presentation of
Wilhelm and Adler is further in evidence in the presentation of
Tamkin. A slightly hideous figure, a character recognizably out
of the world of Bellow's grotesque eccentrics, Tamkin's philosophy consolidates and augments Wilhelm's sensitive intimation
as to the true nature of humanity. However, his behaviour profoundly contradicts his ideas. Stressing the value of love and
the need to "seize the day" (p. 66) and transcend the ugliness of
the business world, Tamkin is simultaneously engaged in
swindling Wilhelm out of his last savings.

In *Seize the Day* Bellow seems to want to affirm the value of
"feelings," but the vessels for his most-cherished ideas are the
childish Wilhelm and the grotesque and eccentric Tamkin.
Moreover, and most important, in *Seize the Day* the symbolic
alignment of the hero with babies, feebleminded children, sensitive women, homosexuals, fools, idiots, Romantic poets and
other people who display their feelings is quite unmistakeable.
Bellow constantly implies that whatever he is, Tommy Wilhelm
is not a recognizable brand of adult American male. Indeed,
Wilhelm himself is plagued by self-doubts that seem to emanate
from his own suspicion that in his personality and in his behavior he is not all that a grown man should be. For this reason
Wilhelm finds it extremely difficult to act meaningfully or effectively within the adult, male business world that he inhabits.

To a varying degree all of Bellow's heroes feel themselves to
be social impotents: some are worried by this and others are
not. Unfortunately for Wilhelm, unlike the chirpy Augie
March or the self-ironizing Herzog, he is, like Asa Leventhal,
full of the solemnity of complaint. Having, on Tamkin's advice,
gambled the last of his savings on lard stocks in the Chicago
commodities market, Wilhelm expects his father to pick up his
hotel bill for him; having abandoned his wife and two children
and taken up with a mistress (the shadowy Olive, whose presence in the novel is something of a mystery), Wilhelm expects
his wife to stop pressuring him in any way. The fact that
Wilhelm's father is tightfisted and his wife apparently something of a bitch has little relevance in our assessment of
Wilhelm's character. For, internally, he is largely unaffected by
their behavior, drifting along in a fantasy world of his own
making in which he believes bad will change into good without
his having to act.

Wilhelm's history is one of refusal to acknowledge certain truths about himself. An ex-acting extra and ex-salesman, Wilhelm has in the past tried to force his own fantasies upon a resistant reality. At the beginning of the novel, in a sequence that shapes our primary impression of him, Wilhelm painfully recalls how while at college he was picked out by a sleazy talent scout, Maurice Venice, and given a screen test. When the re-sults turned out less than favorable Venice advised Wilhelm to abandon his hopes of stardom and return to school. Unwilling to accept the destruction of his dreams, sick of college, and earnestly determined "to become a man" (p. 15), Wilhelm, after quarreling with his parents, lit out for California. The enter-prise turned out disastrously and Wilhelm spent a few years as an extra before returning to the East Coast. Recalling his changed name (Wilky Adler to Tommy Wilhelm) as the flash-point of his father's animosity towards him, Wilhelm is psycho-logically astute enough to recognize that the change was not only determined by cinematic considerations.

> He had cast off his father's name, and with it his father's opinion of him. It was, he knew it was, his bid for liberty, Adler being in his mind the title of the species, Tommy the freedom of the person. But Wilky was his inescapable self. (P. 25)

The childish Wilky is Tommy's "inescapable self," and Wilhelm depressingly asserts that "there's really very little that a man can change at will" (p. 24). Wilhelm's bids for freedom and to "become a man" are almost perversely designed to gratify his own self-destructive impulses and, consequently his desire to remain a child.

> He invariably took the course he had rejected innumerable times. . . . He had decided that it would be a bad mistake to go to Hollywood, and then he went. He had made up his mind not to marry his wife, but ran off and got married. He had resolved not to invest money into Tamkin, and then had given him a cheque. (P. 23)

In each case Wilhelm has acted against the better advice of his father and it is almost as if he were desperately trying to be the fool that his mean-spirited father has long ago cast him as. "You fool, you clunk, you Wilky!" (p. 25), he thinks to himself as if once named, his idiotic fate was sealed. However, Wilhelm's behavior displays a certain recklessness, and paradoxically a trust in humanity that his father's cautious behavior can never acknowledge.

Nevertheless, it is Wilhelm's childishness that primarily recommends itself to us. Both Dr. Adler and Dr. Tamkin treat Wilhelm, the way he seems to demand to be treated—as if he were a child. The fact that after many years he is back under his father's roof (p. 27) confirms his regression. The manner in which Dr. Adler talks to his son "just nonsense and kid's talk Wilky" (p. 37) is extremely paternalistic—he harshly reprimands him for taking too many pills—and while the "good father," Dr. Tamkin, has a kindlier manner, he is equally paternalistic.

> Take my word. I've made a study of the guilt-aggression cycle which is behind it. I ought to know *something* about that. Straighten your collar. (P. 64)

Wilhelm's wife, Margaret, tells him, "You've got to stop thinking like a youngster" (p. 112), referring both to Wilhelm's refusal to take on adult responsibilities and his naive belief that everything will always be magically made "smooth" (p. 114) for him.

Daniel Weiss has suggested that throughout the novella, Wilhelm is attached to a series of surrogate fathers, "Maurice Venice, the Rojax Corporation, Tamkin, Mr. Perls and Mr. Rappaport."[2] However, unlike Augie March, who slips in and out of "parental" conflicts and seems to give equal weight to each of his "Oedipal" struggles, Tommy Wilhelm does not in fact seem particularly attached to anyone except his own father and Tamkin. The effects on Wilhelm's psyche of his extended and acrimonious struggle with his father are, however, profound. For, rather than search out numerous surrogate fathers (Tamkin is quite enough), Wilhelm tends to merely identify any figure of authority with his own father—and then do his best to avoid them.

Wilhelm's relationship with Mr. Rappaport (with whom he has no rapport whatsoever) is a case in point. Rappaport plays the commodities market where Tamkin and Wilhelm spend much of their time. Wilhelm constructs a fantasy around what he knows of Rappaport in order to be able to identify him with his own father.

He's almost blind, and covered with spots, but this old man still makes money in the market. Is loaded with dough, probably. And I bet he doesn't give his children any. Some of them must be in their fifties. This is what keeps middle-aged men as children. He's master over the dough. (Pp. 101–2)[3]

Wilhelm on his own father is similarly critical, but has more evidence to go on.

But he raged once more against his father. Other people with money, while they're still alive, want to see it do some good. . . . Dad thinks I'm too simple. But I'm not as simple as he thinks. (P. 56)

As he meditates on his father's witholding of funds and affection, Wilhelm thinks, "I wouldn't turn to Tamkin if I could turn to him" (p. 10), but the need to turn to one of the two "fathers" is a vital one and Wilhelm never conceives of a life without "paternal" dependency.

Symbolically, our sense of Wilhelm's prolonged childhood is reinforced by the fact that even in his job as a salesman he has been associated with "childish things": " 'Kiddies' furniture. Little chairs, rockers, tables, Jungle gyms, slides, swings [and] seesaws" (p. 35), that he has sold for the Rojax company.

In *Seize the Day,* Bellow thus expends some energy on undercutting any sympathy that he may be generating for Tommy Wilhelm by making him a "feeling" person. I even suspect that one of Dr. Adler's nastiest insinuations about Wilhelm is being half-humorously shored up by the symbolic exigencies of the text. Questioning Wilhelm about the breakup of his marriage, Adler asks

"Was there a scandal—a woman?"
Wilhelm fiercely defended himself. "No, Dad, there wasn't any woman. I told you how it was."
"Maybe it was a man, then," the old man said wickedly.
Shocked, Wilhelm stared at him with burning pallor and dry lips. (P. 51)

But Wilhelm wears shirts made by Jack Fagman (p. 5), and *Seize the Day* is a novella in which every word seems carefully chosen.

As far as Adler is concerned, Wilhelm's greatest failing is the fact that he "indulges himself too much in his emotions" (p. 47).

Adler, as Wilhelm interprets for us, connects control over one's feelings with growing up.

> Granted, he shouldn't support me. But have I ever asked him to do that? . . . It isn't the money, but only the assistance, not even the assistance, but just the *feeling*. But he may be trying to teach me that a grown man should be cured of such feeling. Feeling got me in dutch at Rojax. I had the *feeling* that I belonged to the firm, and my *feelings* were hurt when they put Gerber in over me. (P. 56)

Given Bellow's characterization of Wilhelm, Adler's ideas do not seem particularly wild. However, if Bellow appears to go to great lengths to convince the reader that it is indeed childish to live off your "feelings," he goes to even greater lengths to discredit anyone like Dr. Adler who has the temerity to say so.

Dr. Adler's rational discourse and hard-nosed realism are set in direct opposition to his son's "feelings." Representing, in addition, the virtues of order and cleanliness, Adler seems all that Wilhelm is not.

> This was what people said: "That's old Professor Adler, who used to teach internal medicine. He was a diagnostician, one of the best in New York, and had a tremendous practice. Isn't he a wonderful looking old guy. It's a pleasure to see such a fine old scientist, clean and immaculate. He stands straight and understands every single thing you say. He still has all his buttons." (Pp. 11–12)

This opening description of Adler serves not only to stress the overt difference between father and son—Adler stands straight, Wilhelm is hunched. Adler is clean and immaculate, his son slovenly—but also to ironize the father's professional abilities. For it is clear from the relationship he has with his son that Adler has no knowledge whatsoever of "internal medicine," that is, he does not understand the yearnings of Wilhelm's soul (Tamkin, by contrast, is deeply interested in the soul). Adler cannot "diagnose" his son's condition, as he is unable to reach out of the selfish net that he has caught himself up in. The fact that he is a "fine old scientist" aligns him with a rationalistic world view that cannot tolerate Tommy's "feelings"; and the fact that he still has "all his buttons" symbolically contrasts his tightness (both fiscal and emotional) with Wilhelm's openess and vulnerability.

> The rain had dribbled from Wilhelm's deformed, transparent raincoat; the buttons of his shirt, which always seemed tiny, were partly broken, in pearly quarters of the moon. . . . (Pp. 59–60)

Dr. Adler is an egotist, and like "the Grandma Lausches, the Mrs. Renlings, and the Lucy Magnuses" of Augie March's world he is "against love" (*The Adventures of Augie March*, p. 410). He cannot even remember the date of his wife's death, something which his son finds upsetting and symbolic of his father's unremitting self-centeredness.

Irredeemably selfish, Adler's personality casts a shadow on the values that he upholds. His monstrous ego actively obscures his son's desperation and prevents the reader from sympathetically identifying with his desire to be left alone. The "realistic" Adler who thinks he sees the world for what it is cannot discern even the most obvious truths about his son just as his son who is supposedly full of "feelings" is insensitive to his father's needs. "Reality" as we perceive it through its exponent, Dr. Adler, does indeed appear to be the uncompromising place that Tamkin and Wilhelm image it as. Bellow's method is thus to alienate the reader from each character in turn and simultaneously to corrode the legitimacy of their ideas about the world. Adler cannot respond to Wilhelm, and Wilhelm although he momentarily acknowledges that his father "with some justice, wanted to be left in peace" (p. 43), cannot let the eighty-year-old man remain unbothered by his childish son.

Bellow's presentation of Wilhelm and of Adler is ambivalent, but the nature of the opposition between father and son is clear. Wilhelm's relationship with Tamkin in the second half of the novella, is somewhat, but not a great deal murkier. Again though, as with Adler and Wilhelm, Tamkin is characterized in a highly ambivalent way.

Tamkin's involvement with Wilhelm prefigures that of Dahfu's with Henderson in *Henderson the Rain King*. In both instances an eccentric figure magically appears to offer the hero advice when he is in despair. The whole episode with Tamkin is dreamlike, almost as if Tamkin were an element of

Wilhelm's imagination rather than an actual character. Tamkin
we soon learn is "wizard-like . . . secret, potent," a "benevolent
magician" (p. 81). Tamkin has Wilhelm under a "hypnotic
spell" (p. 96). Under this spell Wilhelm has handed over his
money to Tamkin for investment in commodities but has also
had his latent passion for poetry reawakened.

> Under Dr. Tamkin's influence Wilhelm had recently begun to
> remember the poems he used to read. . . . He didn't like to
> think about his college days but if there was one course that
> now made sense it was Literature 1. (P. 12)

Throughout the novel Wilhelm's thoughts are interspersed
with snippets of poetry that keep coming back to him "involun-
tarily" (p. 12) from his childhood schooling and college days.
The quotes, from Shakespeare, Milton's *Lycidas,* Shelley, and
Keats are of a fairly uniform "Romantic" nature. That Tamkin
has been instrumental in bringing these lost quotations to light
is indicative of the role he plays in shoring up Wilhelm's faith in
the legitimacy of "feelings." It also suggests Tamkin's own sen-
sitivity and sets him in direct opposition to the philistine Dr.
Adler. However, literary quotations are not Tamkin's only spe-
ciality and the contradictions in his personality are playfully
and skillfully suggested in the depths of Bellow's paranomasial
diction, for, Tamkin is equally obsessed with stock-market quotations.

Neither "here" nor "there," Tamkin is difficult to pin down.
Discussing his slipperiness with Wilhelm, Rubin the news ven-
dor remarks

> "I can't quote him. Who could? You know the way Tamkin
> talks. Don't ask me. Do you want the *Trib.* Aren't you going to
> look at the closing quotations?" (Pp. 7–8)

The difficulty with "quoting" Tamkin, the reason he cannot
be pinned down, is that it is impossible to decide which side of
the fence he is really on. We do not know whether he is a
business charlatan out to milk Wilhelm, or a Romantic
philosopher helping him to penetrate life's truths. Tamkin
forcefully exists on both sides of the fence; he is equally engaged with poetic and business quotations. Bellow's symbolism
subtly conveys Tamkin's dual allegiances. When Tamkin hands

Wilhelm a poem of his own, it is leafed in with a bundle of papers relating to business transactions.

He took out a substantial bundle of onion skin papers and said, "These are receipts of the transactions. . . . And here is a copy of a poem I wrote yesterday." (P. 73)

Tamkin is a grotesque figure, and, as with Adler and Wilhelm, his appearance and his behavior undermine his ideas. Unlike Adler, though, Tamkin's philosophy is rather an attractive one. During a breakfast conversation, Tamkin treats Wilhelm to a lesson from the master.

"With me," said Dr. Tamkin, "I am at my most efficient when I don't need the fee. When I only love. Without a financial reward. I remove myself from the social influences. Especially money. The spiritual compensation is what I look for. Bringing people into the here-and-now. The real universe. . . . Only the present is real. . . . Seize the day." (P. 66)

For the reader, Bellow's presentation of Tamkin's advice is heavily charged with ironic overtones, as Tamkin is about to assist Wilhelm in his endeavor to transcend the material by relieving him of his last savings. However, it is the emphasis that he places on love and spirit as the real reality (which recalls Augie and anticipates Henderson and Herzog) that excites Wilhelm.

Like Augie, Wilhelm considers himself to be on the side of love against all those, like his wife and father, who are, from his point of view, interested only in power. Yet, his needs for love and to love are frustrated at every point. As a result Wilhelm is hard put to hold onto his faith in love as a governing principle in life. Still, rather than sacrifice his ideas about the world, Wilhelm prefers to deny any universal validity to his own experience. Feeling that New York is a place where "the fathers were no fathers and the sons no sons" (p. 90) and "every man spoke a language entirely his own" (ibid), Wilhelm suddenly castigates himself for his own myopic vision.

When you are like this, dreaming that everybody is outcast, you realize that this must be one of the small matters. There is a larger body and from this you cannot be separated. . . .

what Tamkin would call the real soul says plain and under-
standable things to everyone. The sons and fathers are themselves. . . . there truth for everybody may be found and
confusion is only temporary. (P. 84)

Tamkin tells Wilhelm what he has been yearning to hear;
namely, that the real world is not the material world governed
by money and the desire for success but rather the world of the
spirit. In this latter world, love is triumphant, and Wilhelm is
united with his fellowman in a "blaze of love" (p. 85). Moreover,
the apparent reality of Wilhelm's relationship with his father
must thereby be a sham. That it is one-sided, that his father is
selfish, tight, and unsympathetic is only the surface reality.
Wilhelm is able at one point to penetrate this "surface" and
arrive at the inner truth. "You love your old man?" Tamkin asks
him, to which he replies

> "Of course I love him. My father. My mother"—As he said
> this there was a great pull at the very center of his soul. . . .
> Wilhelm never identified what struck within him. It did not
> reveal itself. It got away. (Pp. 92–93)

Were Wilhelm possessed of the intellectual abilities of Moses
Herzog he would have had no trouble in identifying this mysterious stranger.

> A man may say "From now on I'm going to speak the truth."
> But the truth hears him and runs away and hides before he's
> even done speaking. (*Herzog,* p. 271)

The "truth" that has struck home but finally evaded Wilhelm is
that beneath the veneer of bitterness and animosity lies the
reality of a "love" for his parents that is strong and deep. So too
with Maurice Venice, the film agent who turns out to be a faker
who is actually engaged in running a call-girl operation. When
Wilhelm discovers this, he is "unwilling to believe anything very
bad about Venice. Perhaps he was foolish and unlucky a fall
guy, a dope, a sucker" (p. 24).
   In every area of Wilhelm's experience, the "reality" is dirtier
than he would like to believe and he is obliged to make a leap of
faith in order to penetrate to what he considers to be the true
reality where all is harmony and love. Tamkin exists in the

former world and projects the latter and Wilhelm is thus able to solidly identify with him.

Like Augie March, whose vision of setting up an "academy-foster home" must of necessity remain a pipe dream, Wilhelm is doomed to remain cut off from the world of love. In *Augie March* it is the hero's character that seems to prevent him from realizing his dreams; in *Seize the Day* the whole notion of a harmonious world existing contemporaneously with the unpleasant "real" world is called into question.

Seize the Day not only pits father against son, but also the world of business against the world of the spirit, the world of everyday reality against the world elsewhere. In local terms, what this comes down to is Wilhelm's personalized version of the country versus the city: his dreams of escape to his little Roxbury garden where he can "breathe in the sugar of the pure morning" (p. 82).

> In late spring weather . . . he used to sit expanded in a wicker chair with the sunlight pouring through the weave . . . young hollyhocks . . . small flowers. This peace (he forgot this time had had its trouble too). This peace was gone. (P. 43)

For a few moments here, Bellow is close to affirming that nice gardens are the antidote to horrible cities—that Romanticism triumphs over Realism—but the narratorial comment puts us right. Wilhelm may have forgotten that he carries his troubles around with him wherever he goes, but we are not permitted the flash of amnesia.

Interestingly, throughout the novel the narrative voice images the world of the city and the business world in particular as "against nature." In the New York commodity market, the board that displays the latest Chicago prices whirrs "like a swarm of electrical bees" (p. 87) and sounds "like a huge cage of artificial birds" (p. 81). That this commercial Byzantium is "against nature" is, of course, what Tamkin has been telling Wilhelm all along—but Bellow never really wants to convince us that there is a balmy and healing world elsewhere. Like Asa Leventhal who tends to lay the blame for his problems on the city rather than on himself. Tommy Wilhelm seems sadly deluded when he puts his faith in "nature."

Tamkin's therapeutic advice to problem-ridden personalities

such as Wilhelm is to "seize the Day." Tamkin envisages man as
isolate and in despair

> I understand what it is when the lonely person begins to feel
> like an animal. When the night comes and he feels like howl-
> ing from his window like a wolf. (P. 67)

Tamkin's vision is of man caught in a conflict between what
he calls the "pretender soul" and the "real soul" (pp. 70–71).
The pretender soul is egotistic and works for the "society mechanism" it "loves" only to aggrandize itself. The real soul, which
wants to love and which loves the truth, balked by the pretender soul, turns into a killer and wants to kill the pretender
soul—the deceiver.

Tamkin's theory seems to restate in different terms what
Freud stated in *Civilization and its Discontents* and what Bellow
states (if only to deny) in so many novels: that is, that the cause
of man's unhappiness is his necessary submission to the demands of civilization, what Tamkin calls the "society mechanism." The real soul cannot triumph if there is to be society,
and, naturally once again its "balked longings come back as
stinging poison" (*Herzog*, p. 232). Tommy Wilhelm is a case in
point. Frustrated in his attempts to receive and give love,
Wilhelm's love turns to hate. When he begins to choke himself
in front of his father in order to demonstrate the effect that his
wife is having on him, we have a sense that it is actually what he
would like to be doing to her.

Interestingly, Wilhelm attributes his own misfortunes to his
inability to discover an outlet for his energy. Early in the novel
we learn that

> he had been slow to mature, and he had lost ground, and so
> he hadn't been able to get rid of his energy and he was
> convinced that this energy itself had done him the greatest
> harm. (P. 7)

It is tempting to conceive of this energy as the mass of
Wilhelm's impulses to break free of his father, and of its turning to poison as the inevitable result of Wilhelm's failure to do
so.

Tamkin envisions most human beings as existing in "a kind of
purgatory. You walk on the bodies. They are all around. I can
hear them cry *de profundis* and wring their hands" (p. 71). When

Tamkin reports this vision to Wilhelm, he is horrified and can only retort by pathetically reasserting his faith in the redeeming powers of nature.

> Well . . . there are also kind, ordinary, helpful people. They're out in the country. . . . (P. 72)

To a certain extent Augie March shares Wilhelm's idea of the joys of country life, but *Seize the Day* is a bleaker work than *Augie March* and there is no omniscient narrator to put Augie's fantasies into proper perspective.

Tamkin, like the true quack that he is, does offer Wilhelm a remedy for his troubles. It is contained in the rather obscure poem that he hands him during one of their conversations. Called "Mechanism vs. Functionalism, Ism vs. Hism" (p. 75), Tamkin's poem opposes "being" and "egotism." The poem urges its addressee (evidently Wilhelm) to penetrate beneath the surface reality of the world

> Seek ye then that which are not there
> In thine own glory let thyself rest.
>
> (P. 75)

Tamkin's particular *carpe diem,* on which the poem is a gloss, actually recommends transcendence of the material world and arrival in the world of love. Naturally he makes no attempt whatsoever to follow his own advice; his behavior is in direct contradiction to his philosophy and he is involved in the shadiest of business dealings. Wilhelm, desperately searching for a way out of the world's business, fails to grasp the meaning of Tamkin's poem, but does, paradoxically, manage a moment of transcendence, at the novel's end.

Tricked by Tamkin, Wilhelm arrives at the commodities market only to discover he has been wiped out financially. In a desperate state, penniless, and metaphorically "stripped naked" (p. 117), Wilhelm fruitlessly searches for Tamkin. Returning to his hotel and failing to find Tamkin in his room, Wilhelm makes one final attempt to save himself by appealing to his father. Rejected in the most brutal fashion, Wilhelm finds himself out on the street where, suddenly, he thinks he catches sight of Tamkin disappearing into a funeral chapel. Pursuing his quarry, Wilhelm is caught up in the crowd outside and carried in among the mass of mourners. Once inside he ap-

proaches the coffin, and the sight of the dead man finally re-
leases all Wilhelm's pent-up emotions and frustrations.

> Soon he was past words, past reason, coherence. . . . the
> source of all tears had suddenly sprung open within him,
> black, deep and hot and they were convulsing his body. . . . he
> cried with all his heart. (Pp. 117–18)

Drowning in his own tears, Wilhelm achieves a momentary
transcendence.

> The flowers and lights fused ecstatically in Wilhelm's blind
> wet eyes; the heavy sea-like music came up to his ears. It
> poured into him where he had hidden himself in the center
> of a crowd by the great and happy oblivion of tears. He heard
> it and sank deeper than sorrow toward the consummation of
> his heart's ultimate need. (P. 118)

As Allen Guttmann has noted, "Almost every commentator
on *Seize the Day* has seen the conclusion as a rebirth," and I
would add, as incorporating an affirmation of humanity in the
face of death.[4] For Keith Opdahl, Wilhelm, in the Jewish funeral home,

> accepts his racial heritage; before the corpse of a stranger he
> accepts his human heritage.[5]

Tony Tanner's analysis elegantly combines the critical view-
points of many of the critics who came after him.

> What is he weeping for? Many things coalesce in his tears.
> The dead man is a reminder of the inevitable death of the
> self, at the same time he is a very specific omen to Tommy,
> helpless and friendless on this day of reckoning. Tommy's
> tears are for humanity and for himself. Yet they also reveal
> an awareness of the supreme value of life, sheer life itself,
> existing beyond the assessment of financial success or fail-
> ure.[6]

I would suggest that the man in the coffin calls up not only
Wilhelm's "dying self" and "humanity" but more specifically
Wilhelm's father and Tamkin. Wilhelm's last meeting with his
father takes place in the morguelike massage basement of the
Hotel Gloriana, while it is Tamkin who has supposedly disap-

peared into the funeral chapel never to appear again. Wilhelm, at the end of the novel, "stripped naked" has lost both his fathers. He is metaphorically an orphan. Adler's parting words to his son are

> "You want to make yourself into my cross. But I am not going to pick up a cross. I'll see you dead, Wilky, by Christ, before I let you do that to me."
> "Father, listen! Listen!"
> "Go away from me now. It's torture for me to look at you, you slob!" cried Dr. Adler. (P. 110)

The play on Christ's passion signifies Wilhelm's sense of total abandonment. Both father and surrogate father betray and reject their son. Wilhelm's "mourning" in the funeral parlour signals an unwanted "birth" into manhood, but rather than accepting it and rather than arriving in "reality" when the spell of both fathers is broken, Wilhelm apparently floats up and embraces what Tanner et al call an affirmation of "sheer life itself" and what I would call a denial of sheer reality itself.[7]

Wilhelm cries because he has been made an "orphan" and also because he identifies with the dead man—not so much because he will one day die, but because with his "fathers" dead to him, he is also, to a large extent, dead himself. Unwilling to grow up and unable to define himself except in opposition or submission to his "fathers" Wilhelm has no "being" when he is disconnected from them. If sinking "deeper than sorrow" suggests that Wilhelm's tears are also tears of joy it can only be because he has imaged the death of his oppressors. Such death, is, however, a two-edged sword.

In *Seize the Day,* everyday reality is depicted in uncompromising terms, and the possibility of transcending the problems of what Wilhelm calls "the world's business" is mooted and dismissed. Daniel Weiss has suggested that, faced with overwhelming problems, Tommy Wilhelm's greatest desire is to return to the womb.[8] It is perhaps significant that in his next novel Bellow sent his hero back, not to his mother's womb, but to its closest approximation—the womb of mankind, Africa. As in *Seize the Day,* in *Henderson the Rain King* the hero is desperate to be reborn.

Part Three_____

Anywhere Out of This World

6_____

Henderson the Rain King

Mary Douglas's seminal work on primitive and contemporary concepts of pollution and taboo, *Purity and Danger,* begins by demonstrating how, for us, as for "primitives," "dirt is essentially disorder."[1] According to Douglas, dirt is a relative concept exemplified by, say, the unease that is caused in an individual by the presence of clean gardening tools in his or her bathroom. What we are trying to do when we "chase dirt" is creative, an attempt "to relate form to function, to make unity of experience. . . ."[2] For

> ideas about separating, purifying, demarcating and punishing transgressions have as their main function to impose system on an inherently untidy experience. It is only by exaggerating the difference between within and without, above and below, male and female, with and against, that a semblance of order is created. . . .
> . . . *reflection on dirt involves reflection on the relation of order to disorder,* being to non-being, form to formlessness, life to death. Wherever ideas of dirt are highly structured their analysis discloses a play upon such profound themes.[3]

The rituals of "primitive" tribes are thus designed to establish "order" in much the same way as some of our governing "civilized" codes of behavior.

As understood by Douglas, any cohesive society or community is founded on order. Douglas shows how rituals of separation function as a means of forcing a society to keep its form in mind rather than (or as well as) helping it to avoid any real or active pollution. "Primitive" man is thus as unhappily "civilized" as his "advanced" contemporary. Tribal taboos on incest are formed by the same principles as tribal rituals involving the eating of excrement—that the former is to us "civilized" and the latter "primitive" is meaningless in that the eating of excrement is only relatively different from our own excremental "rituals"—its ritual purpose being to create *order*. For Douglas, the "primitive" society is, in this fundamental way, paradigmatic of civilized society.

If Douglas's book seems to come into this study of Bellow from nowhere, it parallels the appearance of *Henderson the Rain King* in Bellow's canon. On the surface, anyway, *Henderson* is a maverick work, featuring as it does one of the two gentile protagonists in Bellow's fiction and Bellow's only nonurban landscape. However, both Douglas's book and *Henderson the Rain King* center on fundamental "Bellovian" issues, and *Purity and Danger* has particular application to the pseudo-anthropological *Henderson*.

The Africa that Bellow creates for his hero, Eugene Henderson, like the primitive societies that Douglas examines, turns out to be paradigmatic of a contemporary world: in Bellow's case the paradigm is of America as Bellow imagines it in his other novels. In fact, it is not as surprising as it at first appears to be that in *Henderson the Rain King* Bellow chose to abandon the familiar metropolitan world of his other novels and to concentrate his attention on two tribal villages. For, the clearly demarcated world of the "primitive" tribes lends itself to the kind of schematic division to which Bellow's creative imagination is attracted.

The tendency of Bellow's heroes is to regard the world that they inhabit as a place governed by rules and conventions that often appear to be arbitrary or absurd. An imagined "primitive" society thus serves Bellow well, as through it he is able to transform the hidden, protean, and limiting conventions of his America into a set of "visible" and rigid rituals and thus highlight the essential problems of his hero.

Bellow uses the "primitive" societies that he imagines to represent the vital and imprisoning framework of "civilized" society. The two tribes that Henderson visits—the Arnewi and the Wariri—demand of their tribespeople submission to a set of rituals that appear arbitrary and absurd but which apparently secure the continued order and harmony of tribal society. One of the most important lessons that is offered to Henderson while he is in "the womb" of Africa (it should be noted that like Bellow's other heroes, Henderson is "offered" many lessons, all of which he tends to ignore) is that while the rituals of the social world imprison, their abandonment is potentially catastrophic.

In this sense, *Henderson* recapitulates, in a fascinating way, the insights into the relation of ritual (whether "primitive" or "civilized") to order that Douglas achieves through her anthropological approach.

If Bellow uses Africa paradigmatically to represent the painful aspects of everyday life in America, he also uses it, in a more conventional manner, to correspond to the "heart of darkness," the chaotic dark world from which Bellow's heroes are always separated by a hair's breadth: the chasm that Joseph, Leventhal, Wilhelm, and, as we shall see, Henderson are all afraid of falling into. In *Henderson the Rain King*, Bellow's quasi-allegorical Africa thus mirrors aspects of both his hero's external and internal worlds.

Eugene Henderson, on the surface, appears to be a unique Bellow hero. He is the scion of a patrician New England family and a multimillionaire by inheritance. Henderson is thus released from the twin burdens that afflict all of Bellow's other heroes with the exception of Albert Corde—Jewishness and money. Not far beneath the surface, however, Henderson is an immediately recognizable Bellovian type. Like all Bellow's heroes, only more so, Henderson is drawn to an idea of order and afflicted by a propensity to create chaos. He yearns to occupy "a station in life" (p. 34) and at the age of fifty-five contemplates embarking upon a medical career. At the base of his desire to be a doctor is his apparently hereditary "service ideal" (p. 86): a philanthropic urge that moves Henderson to try to help others with their most fundamental social needs. However, Henderson is, of course, incapable of behaving in the kind of social and conventional ways that might allow him to achieve his ideals or realize his fantasies.

Like Augie March, Henderson is sick of striving—which Henderson calls "Becoming" (p. 160)—and he years to settle down—Henderson's term is "to Be" (p. 160). However, in Africa Henderson "learns" that he will not achieve internal order without submitting to a measure of external order. Alternatively, he also "learns" that the only possible way to transcend his society's limiting rules and laws is to enter the heart of darkness, to return to the truly primitive, and this too Henderson is incapable of doing.

The "lessons" that Henderson receives come in two ways: directly, from "mentors" like Prince Itelo and King Dahfu and indirectly from his clashes and engagements with what are to him the incomprehensible rituals of the Arnewi and the Wariri. Again Mary Douglas and Bellow overlap. For, Henderson's conflicts and strivings to discover happiness are explored, via a tribal matrix, in dialectical terms; reflection on these terms invites reflection on "the relation of order to disorder, being to non-being, form to formlessness and life to death." What is more, Henderson's misunderstanding of tribal concepts of pollution is central to *our* understanding of the most basic problems of his existence.

In *Seize the Day* and *The Adventures of Augie March,* the conflict between the forces of order and those of chaos or freedom (terms that are often synonymous in Bellow's canon) is expressed through a conflict of fathers and sons. In *Henderson the Rain King,* it is not the authority of fathers, and all that they represent, that is challenged and tested but, through the paradigm of Henderson's experiences in Africa, the governing conventions of democratic society and the most basic demands of civilization.

Henderson goes to Africa because he hopes it will provide him with an antidote to the misery that he has been experiencing for much of his adult life in America, a misery, which the opening four chapters of the novel reveal, has largely been caused by Henderson's inability to "fit in" on any level of society.

In America Henderson feels himself trapped in a society that can sustain him materially but not spiritually. As the member of an élite class and the descendant of an illustrious family (his "great grandfather was Secretary of State . . . his father was the famous scholar . . . a friend of William James and Henry Adams") (p. 7), Henderson is one of America's "chosen" and yet he feels himself to be almost terminally estranged from his native land. Henderson is materially comfortable, but, unfortunately for him, he is not a materialist. Instead, he is tormented by an inner voice that cries "I want, I want, I want, oh I want. . . ." (p. 12), but that cannot be quieted by anything that capitalist America has to offer. Neither does Henderson find solace in the spiritual fruits of European civilization. On his Connecticut estate he indifferently bulldozes over statues from Florence and Salzburg—priceless works of art brought to the New World by Henderson family money—in order to make way for a pig farm.

Henderson's outlet for his spiritual frustration is physically and mentally to abuse those who are closest to him—his wife, family, and members of the Connecticut community where he lives. At home Henderson behaves like an egotistical monster, treating his wife like a stranger and terrorizing her friends. Away from home, he is no better: he brawls in country saloons, fights with snowplow drivers, gets drunk and rowdy in fancy hotels, and, although he is neither, "always behave[s] like an ignorant man and a bum" (p. 23). Henderson's insatiable longings poison his marriage and threaten to collapse the structure of his entire life. As a last resort, Henderson drives himself forth in the hope of discovering a cure for his ills. After first contemplating a trip to see the Eskimo, he finally decides to light out for Africa.

Is there something wrong with Henderson or with America or with both these oversized entities? At first it seems as if Henderson's quest is a familiar one. In the conventional manner of a Romantic adventurer, he is leaving behind modern society and its burgeoning materialism to go in search of spirit and wisdom. But Henderson's ultimate goals are not those common to the spiritual explorer. Henderson conceives of spiritual regeneration not as an end in itself but as a means to an end. His "service ideal" takes precedence over any inner equilibrium that he might achieve. His heart is set on medical school, but he knows that in his present state, suits, ties and application forms are out of the question.

An egotist of large proportions, the Henderson who sets off for Africa is a man incapable of respecting any limits that are not self-imposed. His quest may thus be paraphrased as an attempt to discover how to achieve order, stability, and place without submitting to the arbitrary and onerous demands of what Henderson conceives to be a spiritually moribund American culture. In Africa, however, Henderson "discovers" a world where spiritual balance is founded on absurdity and death, and where the wisdom that is offered is attainable only at the expense of absurd or cruel rituals. The framework of tribal society is "what is wrong" with American society stripped bare of distracting materialism. Tribal wisdom has it that if you want "order" or to be a part of society, you must pay the ritual price. No Bellow hero likes to hear this news and it is particularly unwelcome to the egotistical Henderson's one good ear. In

terms of mileage, Henderson travels a long way, but Bellow's
Africa turns out to be a place that is not too different from
Bellow's America.

Interestingly, in order to consolidate his allegorical point,
Bellow skillfully reverses his common metaphorical structures
in *Henderson the Rain King* so that a reflexive relationship between "primitive" and "civilized" worlds is maintained. During
the rain ceremony of the Wariri, for example, the roar of the
crowd is

> a great release of sound, like Coney Island or Atlantic City or
> Time Square on New Year's Eve. . . . the frenzy was so great it
> was metropolitan. (P. 169)

Similarly, Henderson's "darkest" African experiences correspond only to his worst experiences in New York

> After the gust of breeze came deeper darkness, like the pun-
> gent heat of the trains when they pass into Grand Central
> tunnel on a devastated day of August, which is like darkness
> eternal. At that moment I have always closed my eyes.
> (P. 200)

Wariri tribesmen are like the "fantastic apparition[s]" that New
York can "throw up behind you" (p. 172), and a royal proces-
sion is similarly evocative.

> And I thought that this was like a summer's day in New York.
> I had taken the wrong subway and instead of reaching Upper
> Broadway I had gone to Lenox Avenue and 125th Street,
> struggling up to the sidewalk. (P. 166)

Bellow's Africa, says Marcus Klein, "has the feel of Chicago and
the smell of New York."[4] However, we must also bear in mind
that Bellow's Chicago and New York often have the feel and
smell of exotic cities like Bangkok, or stretches of the Amazo-
nian jungle or the wide African plains where the light is "yellow
. . . like the slit of the eye of a wild animal, say a lion" (*The Victim*,
p. 51).

While the part of Africa that Henderson visits turns out to be
intermittently metropolitan, it is also imaged as a mysterious
place beyond both geography and history. Romilayu, the guide
who Henderson picks up shortly after his arrival in the dark

continent, offers to take Henderson "far far" into the African interior. The specific location he has in mind is the Hinchagara plateau, a place that "has never been well-mapped" and where "geographically speaking," Henderson doesn't have "the remotest idea" where he is (pp. 44–45).

It is on this remote plateau that Henderson encounters both the Arnewi, who are a passive cattle-loving people, and the Wariri, whose culture is built on magic and death and who are much enamored of lions.

Henderson's approach to the Arnewi village takes him along a dried-up river bed. From a distance, the circular roofs of the Arnewi huts and the smoke that curls from them evoke for Henderson "the original place . . . older than the city of Ur" (p. 47). While Henderson is clearly heading for some ur-experiences, the village itself turns out to be slightly less original than he has imagined. On the outskirts of the village he is surrounded by pot-bellied African children and led to the Arnewi's regal leader, Prince Itelo. Much to Henderson's surprise and ill-concealed disappointment, the prince addresses his visitors in fluent English. Itelo is gracious, charming, and consoling, "You thought first footstep? Something new? I am very sorry. We are discovered" (p. 53). Itelo, it turns out, has learned his English not from white explorers but in a Syrian mission school. He is also the only member of his tribe to have been "exposed" to the civilized world—a world from which he has happily returned to take up his royal duties.

Henderson gives himself a quick slap on the wrist for, however unconsciously, having entertained foolish Livingstoneish fantasies and he hastens to reassure Itelo that he is a spiritual and not a geographic explorer. Before he can begin to plumb "the greater or the deeper facts of life" (p. 54), however, Henderson becomes embroiled in a problem that is threatening to destroy the tribe.

As Henderson should have guessed from the dried-up river bed, the Arnewi are suffering form a terrible drought. Arnewi cattle, whom the tribespeople regard as "relatives" more than domestic animals, are beginning to die in large numbers. A reserve stock of water, held in a large cistern, does exist, but the water is "polluted." That is, an Arnewi taboo forbids the touching of animals that are in the drinking water and, unfortunately, the cistern has been taken over by a thriving community of frogs.

As soon as he becomes acquainted with the dimensions of the problem, Henderson determines to put all to rights by using some Yankee ingenuity (it is not for nothing that Henderson hails from Connecticut). With a great show of bravura he offers to blow the frogs out of the cistern with a homemade bomb. First, however, he reads the prince a short lecture.

I said, "Do you know why the Jews were defeated by the Romans? Because they wouldn't fight back on Saturday. And that's how it is with your water situation. Should you preserve yourself, or the cows, or preserve the custom? I would say yourself. Live," I said "to make another custom. Why should you be ruined by frogs?" The prince listened and said only, "Hm, very interestin, Is that a fact? 'Strodinary." (Pp. 61–62)

Henderson's response to the Arnewi's problems is conditioned by years of rebellious activity back in the States. The passive, "bovine" Arnewi are avatars of Henderson's conventional Connecticut neighbors. Henderson fails to make the connection perhaps because he is distracted by the Arnewi's exoticism, but the parallels are significant. It is, after all, a Dr. Bullock who is most outraged by Henderson's allowing his pigs to run free on a suburban lawn. Henderson upsets his Connecticut neighbors by behaving unconventionally and he is willing to risk upsetting his Arnewi hosts by flying in the face of their rituals.

Henderson refuses to believe that societies can be held together by what appear to be absurd and stupid rules. Does Bellow believe this too? His portrayal of Dr. Bullock and of the Arnewi suggests that he might, for in his dealings with them it is Henderson who has our sympathy. However, when Henderson tries out his bomb he succeeds in blasting out the frogs only at the expense of blowing a hole in the cistern wall and draining away the entire community water supply. If there is a moral here, it is surely one familiar to Bellow's readers: societies' rules and conventions are onerous and potentially deathly, but if you break them, chaos is certain to follow.

The deep rhythm of Henderson's behavior dictates that his attempts to put things (including his own life) in order will end in disaster. At the root of Henderson's need to create chaos, whether conscious or unconscious, is his need to assert himself on his own terms. In this he differs in an important way from

Bellow's other heroes. As Howard Harper has written, "Henderson is caught in the familiar existential dilemma of Bellow's heroes; yearning for order and meaning in his life he finds only chaos and meaninglessness."[5] But, rather than responding to his dilemma by withdrawing from society into a world inside his own head, Henderson clashes directly with his society. Where Bellow's other heroes try in some way to "protect" their autonomous minds from experience, Henderson actively engages with the world—even if his engagements tend to become mere lopsided affirmations of the strength of his own personality.

More egotist than solipsist, Henderson is a social outcast rather than one who has cast himself out. The difference may not be very great in terms of his ultimate "Bellovian dilemma," but it does affect our response to him as a character. For, Henderson is in many ways the most "there" of all Bellow's heroes. Gigantic in size ("Six feet four inches tall, two hundred and thirty pounds" (p. 4), Henderson also has a presence because he "acts out" his discontent with the civilized world. We don't want to see Henderson "curbed" in the way that the discontented Joseph, Leventhal, Wilhelm, and Herzog "curb" themselves, for much of our enjoyment of Henderson comes from our observation of the scrapes that his foolish egotism gets him into. If *Henderson the Rain King* seems a less claustral work than Bellow's other novels, it must be because in this novel we escape the confines of the hero's head with greater frequency. When Henderson blows up the Arnewi's cistern, you can almost hear the explosion reverberate throughout Bellow's canon. For once, repressed longings have not "come back as stinging poison" but have been energetically (if destructively) released.

When Henderson turns the Arnewi's cistern into a dry dock, he quickly transforms himself from a welcome visitor into an enemy of the people—a role he knows well—and he and Romilayu are obliged to make a speedy exit from the village. In the brief period of his stay, however, Henderson has managed to pick up one particularly important insight into "the greater . . . deeper facts of life." During an audience with Itelo's aunt, the old Queen Willatale, Henderson has learned of the "gruntu-molani" (p. 85). This piece of tribal wisdom, literally "Man want to live," is passed onto Henderson first as an assessment of himself but later comes to have more general application as a philosophy. Queen Willatale is a "woman of Bittahness" something which Henderson translates as "Be-er." Moreover she is "not only a woman but a man at the same time" and has "risen above ordinary human limitations" (p. 75). She is thus an appealing personality to the earthbound Henderson, who enviously divides human beings into the Be-ers and the Becomers.

> Being people have all the breaks. Becoming people are very unlucky, always in a tizzy. The Becoming people are always having to make explanations or offer justifications to the Being people. While the Being people provoke these explanations, I sincerely feel that this is something everyone should understand about me. (P. 160)

Henderson feels that "Becoming" is beginning to come out of his ears (p. 160) and that it has exhausted him to such an extent that his inner spirit has gone to sleep.

> Enough! Enough! Time to have become. Time to Be! Burst the spirit's sleep. Wake up America! Stump the experts. (P. 160)

"Wake up America!" says our hero apparently referring to himself and indeed no one has hesitated to identify Henderson's quest with that of the country. For Eusebio Rodrigues, "Henderson has to be seen as the embodiement of mid-twentieth century America, bursting with vital energy, at the very peak of its prosperity" and yet issuing forth "a cry of intense yearning, I want, I want."[6] Norman Podhoretz (again in his preconservative mode) finds Henderson to be "an allegorical personification of the vague malaise, the sense of aimless drift and unused energy, that seems to afflict a prosperous and spiritually stagnant society like our own."[7] However, if, like his country of origin, Henderson is spiritually stagnant and intensely yearning, he is also, in a more particularly Belovian manner, a character who cannot take what he wants—in this case "spirit"—when it is offered to him. Henderson gets excited about the "grun-tu-molani" but he is willing to step along the road to Being only so far.

The conditions for "Being," as Henderson seems aware after the debacle of the cistern, cannot begin to be met while he insists on going his own way. "I hoped to learn the wisdom of life from [Willatale]," says Henderson, "but I guess I am just too rash" (p. 112). Imaginatively and intellectually fired by his restless movement and outrageous behavior and energetically driven by his own brand of dynamic paralysis, Henderson's desire "to Be" seems no more real than Augie March's desire to settle down on a farm.

Henderson moves from the ordered, paradigmatically "bourgeois" world of the Arnewi to that of the Wariri—a very different type of society. Romilayu describes the Wariri as "chillen dahkness" (p. 115) and the travelers' first encounters with the tribesmen bear him out. The Wariri greet Henderson with guns, disarm him, lead him into their village and dump him in a hut that, Henderson soon discovers, is inhabited by a corpse. However, as Henderson discovers the following morning, this village of darkness is presided over by an enlightened king— the remarkable Dahfu. Dahfu is a formidably charismatic figure. Like Itelo he is the lone tribal member to have ventured into the civilized world, but his character reflects an altogether more powerful combination of Western learning and tribal wisdom. Dahfu is literate, cultured, refined, articulate, and possessed of a most eccentric genius. He is also a handsome and athletic figure who exudes nobility.

When Henderson is brought before the king, the two men hit it off immediately. Henderson is excited because Dahfu, relaxed, controlled, "all ease" (p. 160) and "sumptuously at rest" (p. 153), appears to be everything that Henderson is not and would like to be: he is, in fact an African monarch who is a palpable Other. And Dahfu is delighted with his visitor because Henderson quickly reveals himself as the perfect testing ground for some of Dahfu's quirky theories. The surfacing of "quirky theories" should not surprise us. For, while there are elements in Dahfu's personality that link him with the conventional "wise natives" of Rider Haggard's African romances, he, at least as far as his ideas are concerned, belongs in a line of descent from grotesque crackpots like Allbee and Tamkin. Dahfu, it soon turns out, is the master of an idiosyncratic philosophy whose praxis, coincidentally, is designed to restore inner spirit to those who have lost it.

Dahfu's philosophy seems to combine some of the ideas of William James with some of Wilhelm Reich's (the latter is always a Bellow favorite). The basis of his thought is that we are the authors of both our worlds and our own external appearances. Dahfu believes that by altering the inner spirit, the outer world too will be changed. However, while some of Dahfu's ideas are sophisticated and "Western," he still respects magic as a force to be reckoned with. The way to achieve a balanced inner spirit—and Henderson will be the test and proof of this—is to voyage back into the primitive (primal?) self, make contact with the deep, wild, chaotic forces within us, "become" temporarily the animal within and then re-emerge triumphantly transformed into a beauty both within and without.

The particular "therapy" that Henderson is to undergo involves a terryfyingly close encounter with a half-tamed lioness called Atti. Atti's den is in the basement of Dahfu's palace and it is here that Henderson will receive instruction on how to remove his "ego emphasis" (p. 262), how to take "lioness" into himself, and how to "overcome [his] old self" (p. 297).

If Itelo and the Arnewi gave Henderson the message that society may be rejoined only through the front door—that is by paying heed to rules and conventions, Dahfu and the Wariri, less-rigid members of the Institute of Bellovian Psychoanalysis, offer him a chance to reenter through the back door. The road to a restored Henderson, and to the acceptance of order in Connecticut is via a little chaos on the Hinchigara plateau. However, as soon as Dahfu begins to put his plans for Henderson into action, the latter is terrified.

Down in the den, Dahfu casually rides Atti's back while a tearful Henderful quakes and moans. Eventually the time comes for Henderson to enter the heart of darkness and commence his transformation. Henderson manages to get down on his knees and roar for all he is worth while the lion stands idly by—but his heart is not really in it. "For his [Dahfu's] sake I accepted the discipline of being a lion" (p. 297), says Henderson, but a more pressing voice is beginning to tell him that the king is probably more than a little crazy. Henderson turns out to be as chary of lions and real "wildness" as he has been of cows and conventionality. Moreover, Connecticut may be dull, but when Henderson discovers (as he soon does) that the village of the Wariri is a place where justice is arbitrary and ritual murder a commonplace, he is less than pleased.

If we remember that the novel is set in Africa and not California and that Bellow and not Carlos Castaneda is our guide, Henderson's situation quickly reveals itself as a familiar one. A Bellow hero, yearning for a redemptive revelation, has taken up with or been taken up by someone who may be brilliant but who is obviously also a crank. As his lion therapy progresses, Henderson becomes increasingly convinced that Dahfu's genius is "not a secure gift, but like [his] ramshackle palace rested on doubtful underpinnings"[8] (p. 269). Eventually, the terms of Dahfu's instruction lose their relevance altogether. Dahfu imparts the message "Seize The Animal Within" not "Seize the Day" but, as in all Bellow's novels, what "the crank" has to say turns out to be much less interesting than the structure of his relationship with the hero to whom he is saying it.

"The beauty of Dahfu's person prevailed on me as much as his words" (p. 214), says Henderson, who goes on to acknowledge that Dahfu is "dragging [him] along with the power of his personal greatness" (p. 295). Dahfu turns out to be yet another bloodbrother, surrogate father, teacher. However, he is a slightly deviant version of the usual "mentor," as he manages to remain a compelling and attractive figure throughout the novel.

In Bellow's novels there are ugly mentors and beautiful ones. The two most beautiful, and the two for whom the heroes of the novels in which they appear feel the most love, are Dahfu, the philosopher king and Von Humboldt Fleisher, the "poet-king" of *Humboldt's Gift* (p. 25). These characters, unlike the slippery Tamkin *(Seize the Day)*, or the falsely elevated Lausch and Einhorn *(The Adventures of Augie March)*, exude what seems to be a genuine nobility of person. However, at some point even these beautiful mentors must be undercut. If the Bellow hero is to continue "dangling," his options must always gradually close down and anyone like Dahfu or Humboldt, who appears to offer the hero a way out of his dilemma, must, of necessity, be revealed as a monomaniac and a lunatic.

Dahfu and Humboldt share similar flaws in their personalities: both display willfulness of Nietzschean proportions and both are characterized by an ambitiousness that ultimately o'erleaps itself and brings them to their doom. Henderson and Citrine are willing to walk to the edge of the cliff with their respective mentors but once there they will not jump off with them. The problem with all Bellow's mentors is that— Absolutists, Nietzschians, Faustians, Crazy Poets, or whatever— they go too far. Dahfu's particular excess is that he goes too far down paths of darkness. For Henderson, conventional life is figuratively deathly, but Dahfu's magical mystery tours threaten to have death itself as their terminus.

Surprisingly, however, it is not Dahfu's experiments with "lion-ness" that finally kill him, but his rigid adherence to a savage ritual of accession. Wariri custom demands that before Dahfu can be fully confirmed in his kingship, he must trap a wild lion. Not just any old wild lion but a particular animal that supposedly contains the soul of Dahfu's father Gmilo. Henderson tries to warn his friend from attempting such a dangerous activity, but Dahfu points out to Henderson that he cannot switch from the "old universe" to the "new universe" merely when it is convenient for him to do so.

> To Gmilo, the lion Suffo was his father. To me, grandfather. Gmilo, my father. As, if I am going to be king of the Wariri, it has to be. Otherwise, how am I the king? (P. 296)

There are shades here of Itelo and the pollution problem. This time, however, Henderson does not interfere and his worst premonitions are borne out when Dahfu is gruesomely torn to pieces by the lion that he has been trying to capture. If through his death-defying lion therapy, Dahfu has achieved Stillness, Being, and Inner Beauty, he has nevertheless chosen to remain a prisoner of absurd and cruel rituals. If there is a message here for Henderson it is a gloomy one.

Henderson ends up in Africa with much the same feelings that he had in America. He is twice witness to the absurdity of ritual—once with cows and once with lions—and he is also made deeply aware of the danger that is involved in plumbing the depths of one's being. Henderson does not want to accept reality on its own uncompromising terms—these are the rules, please follow them—but neither does he wish to come at reality via his violent, flashing center. Confronted by the "ordered" society of the Arnewi, Henderson is driven to create chaos; confronted by the dark chasms of the Wariri world, Henderson recoils from it in horror.

Norman Mailer once wrote that he "would have been ready to urinate blood" before giving up on "the possibilities of a demonically vast ending" for *Henderson the Rain King*.[9] As far as Mailer is concerned, Bellow "capitulate[s]" when he kills off Dahfu and sends an unregenerated Henderson back to America. But what did Mailer expect? Clearly, he was excited by the presence in a *Bellow* novel of a hero with some Mailer-esque proclivities and by themes that appeared to center on magic, mystery, and death. However, although Mailer doesn't seem to realize it, *all* Bellow's novels are, in his terms, "capitulations."

Bellow's novels do not resolve themselves in the way that Mailer would like, in fact they simply do not resolve themselves. Bellow, it seems to me, must know this, for his endings always have the feel of something tacked on. David Galloway has suggested that it is "because the idea of order, of human solidarity and community, is so important to Bellow [that] he must make some symbolic reaffirmation of that idea in the conclusion of his works." But, as Galloway points out, neither Bellow's plots, nor his central characters are able "to consistently support such gestures."[10]

At the end of *Henderson the Rain King,* we find Henderson on his way back home—somewhat chastened, but not a wiser man (in Khartoum he even manages a brief but characteristic run-in with the U.S. consular authorities). The plane carrying Henderson on the last leg of his journey makes a stop, symbolically enough, in Newfoundland. Henderson steps out into the icy air and begins to run in circles on the runway. With him is a small orphan boy he has made friends with on the flight and a lion cub, secreted from the Wariri and supposedly containing the soul of Dahfu. Together they go "running—leaping, leaping, pounding, and tingling over the pure white lining of the gray Arctic silence" (p. 341). Bellow leaves us with this lyric moment, a profoundly beautiful image of love and friendship. This, he seems to suggest, is Henderson's new found land. But the epiphany is hardly earned.[11]

7

Herzog

Herzog is a novel about a man freeing himself from a paralyzing obsession with his ex-wife. Almost all of the action takes place inside Moses Herzog's head as he spends a week and a half in feverish thought going over the breakup of his marriage and all its contingent elements: betrayals, lies, child-custody problems, alimony, untrustworthy shrinks, bad friends, deceitful lawyers, conspiring relatives. Painful stuff all of it—or is it?

The opening line of *Herzog* gives us an indication that things may, in fact, be changing for Bellow's burdened and struggling heroes. "If I am out of my mind it's all right with me" (p. 1), thinks Moses Herzog, which seems to be good news as it certainly has not been all right for the five heroes who have preceded him in Bellow's canon. From Joseph through Henderson, a craziness induced by crisis (and vice versa) rends Bellow's heroes to quite devastating effect, but although Moses Herzog suffers in much the same way as his forebears (almost everyone he knows cheats and betrays him), he seems to be enjoying himself. As he himself puts it, "Moses, suffering, suffered in style" (p. 16).

It is hard to know what precipitated this slight but important shift in Bellow's realization of his hero's consciousness and in its relation to the matter of his life—perhaps Bellow simply grew tired of all that endless striving—but its effect is to remove a great weight from Bellow's later fiction. "Was he a clever man or an idiot?" (p. 3), is Herzog's opening question to himself, a familiar one for a Bellow hero to ask, but the answer Herzog provides in the novel is less common. What a shock it is to hear Herzog describe himself as a "child-man" (p. 266), "an eager, hasty, self-intense and comical person" (p. 110), "a frail, hopeful lunatic" (p. 106) suffering from "monstrous egotism" (p. 250), and to see him ironically present himself as a "pure heart in the burlap of innocence" with whom "everyone must be indulgent" (p. 266).

Before the critic has sharpened his pencil, Herzog is bringing himself "to consider his character. What sort of character was it? Well, in the modern vocabulary, it was narcissistic; it was masochistic; it was anachronistic" (p. 4). In the opening six chapters of this book, I somberly deduced these characteristics in Bellow's other heroes and suggested that they contributed to the bleak atmosphere of Bellow's novels. But here is Herzog, evincing a detached gaiety, hanging his personality on the line, "knowing" everything about himself, and, apparently, not giving a damn.

Periodically in the novel, Herzog enacts a session of self-analysis that seems to parody a real analysis. Lying supine on a couch in his Manhattan apartment, Herzog apparently instructs his mind to roll free. But, unlike, say, the analysis in that other great self-consumptive novel of the 1960s, *Portnoy's Complaint,* Herzog's presentation of self is altogether protective.

> Resuming his self-examination, he admitted that he had been a bad husband—twice. Daisy, his first wife, he had treated miserably. Madeleine, his second, had tried to do *him* in. To his son and his daughter he was a loving but bad father. To his own parents he had been an ungrateful child. To his country, an indifferent citizen. To his brothers and sister, affectionate but remote. With his friends an egotist. With love, lazy. With brightness, dull. With power, passive. With his own soul, evasive. (Pp. 4–5)

All this sounds reasonable enough when set in the measured tones of Bellow's ingenuous protagonist (as opposed to the hysterical ones of Roth's Alexander Portnoy). Moreover, although we learn that Herzog is "[s]atisfied with his own severity [and] positively enjoying the hardness and factual rigor of his judgment" (p. 5), we never feel like pillorying Herzog either for his familial irresponsibility of his self-satisfied posing. Herzog soon emerges as "our hero," a beleaguered, sympathetic, attractive personality. Bellow carefully manipulates our response to Herzog's self-criticism and we tend to feel—well, let's just wait and see what these brothers, sisters, friends, and ex-wives are *really* like before we decide who treated whom miserably.[1]

Herzog's emotional problems seem to engage him on some upper level of his mind where they no longer hurt. But it is the way in which he has got them up there that proves to be central to our understanding of the novel. Herzog's marital crisis has somehow "heightened his perceptions" (p. 278), and it has also stimulated him in other ways.

> What I seem to do, thought Herzog, is to inflame myself with my own drama, with ridicule, failure, denunciation, distortion, to inflame myself voluptuously, aesthetically, until I reach a sexual climax. And that climax looks like a resolution and an answer to many higher problems. (P. 208)

Conceiving of himself as an "industry that manufacture[s] personal history" (p. 3), Herzog is an essentially autonomous institution imaginatively geared up by his personal crises and sustained by the wildly complex intellectual figurations that his sexual sublimations throw up. He is, in fact, Bellow's most sophisticated alchemist of crisis: his narrative turns the dross of a tawdry and troubled personal life into a platform for the discussion of everything from German existentialism to Russian mysticism, Calvinism, and Black Muslims, and everyone from Montaigne and Pascal to Kant, Fichte, Nietzsche, Spengler, Heidegger, Eisenhower, Adlai Stevenson, and Martin Luther King, Jr.

In a lengthy series of highly charged mental letters, Herzog writes to "the newspapers, to people in public life, to friends and relatives . . . to the dead, his own obscure dead, and finally the famous dead" (p. 1). His performance is quite dazzling; thoughts, associations, grand and petty ideas run, leap, pound, and tingle through his brain with astonishing rapidity. It is all wonderful stuff for the reader—but are we supposed to take Herzog's ideas seriously, or more seriously than his emotional troubles?

If one idea is uppermost in Herzog's mind, it seems to be that people who live by ideas need debunking. Herzog's own ideas, as he acknowledges, are the flotsam and jetsam of a troubled mind—superfluities, distractions. The intellectual motions that he goes through are graceful, humorous, to the point—*"Dear Doktor Professor Heidegger, I should like to know what you mean by the expression 'the fall into the quotidian.' When did this fall occur? Where were we standing when it happened?"* (p. 49)—but they are a sideshow.

Herzog's ultimate goal is a kind of transcendental peace, an inner and outer quietness: he yearns to still the babble of tongues inside him, to rid his mind of clutter and to exorcise the ghosts of his disastrous marriage. If doing so takes him by way of nineteenth- and twentieth-century German existential theories that he must ponder and discredit before he can dismiss, than so be it.

In its own way *Herzog* is a *Portnoy's Complaint* for intellectuals. The figures in the nightmare—who also provide the entertainment—are not two lower-middle-class Jewish parents with medieval ideas about propriety and *kashrut,* but a whole set of book-crazy movers and shakers—shrinks, lawyers, and academics who have linked arms in Herzog's head with a band of heavyweight philosophers and theologians. In terms of substance, however, nothing of what these pundits and thinkers have to say is of any deeper relevance to Moses Herzog than Sophie Portnoy's meditations on the uncertain properties of the doughnut are to her wayward son.

If neither Herzog's emotional problems nor his intellectual wrangling solidify into anything more than the shiny, brittle surface of the novel, what is it that gives the book its depth? "My novel," Bellow once wrote, "deals with the humiliating sense that results from the American mixture of private concerns and intellectual interests. . . . To me a significant theme of *Herzog* is the imprisonment of the individual in a shameful and impotent privacy. . . . He comes to realize at last that what he has considered his intellectual privilege has proved to be another form of bondage. Anyone who misses this misses the point of the book."[2] Herzog himself makes the same point another way. "Herzog . . . by accepting the design of a *private life* (approved by those in authority) turned himself into something resembling a concubine" (p. 188). Here, as elsewhere, "private life" and all its attendant sexual wranglings is imaged by Herzog as the outlet for "public" and "political" energies that have been frustrated. In other times a man as smart as Herzog would not have been superfluous.

What was he hanging around for? To follow this career of *personal relationships* until his strength at last gave out? Only to be a smashing success in the private realm, a king of hearts? Amorous Herzog, seeking love . . . But this is a female pursuit. This hugging and heartbreak is for women. The occu-

pation of a man is duty, in use, in civility, in politics in the
Aristotelian sense. (P. 94)

It is not always an intelligent move to take issue with a living
author about the themes of his own book, and indeed *Herzog*
does make the point that Bellow claims for it. However, it seems
to me that Herzog, cut off as he is from the world of public
usefulness, suffers a deeper imprisonment than that of
confinement to the private life. The opposition that Bellow sets
up between private and public worlds—an opposition that he
claims derives from the American refusal to treat intellectual
men as responsible adults who can be trusted with power—
actually seems to be a variation of the more idiosyncratic (and
paradoxically more generalized) struggles of all Bellow's heroes
with authority, adulthood, "order," and "civilization." Herzog,
like all his predecessors is doomed by his recalcitrant personality to forever attack the objects of his own desire. His "intellectual privilege" may well be a form of bondage but it also proves
to be abundant compensation for the terrible paralysis involved
in acting out Bellow's version of the human condition. It is in
fact the tension between the familiar "deep structure" of Bellow's novels and its pyrotechnic surface (the manifestations of
Herzog's intellectual privilege) that make *Herzog* at once so
frustrating and so compelling.

The deep contradictions in Herzog's personality are revealed
to us through his extended ruminations on his personal history.
Through them we learn that, though he is a middle-aged
academic who has searched for order in his life, Herzog has
repeatedly acted in such a way as to ensure that he will find only
chaos. Employed in a "perfectly respectable" (p. 5) secure, ten-
ured, academic position, Herzog has, when we meet him, given
up his job in favor of part-time night-school teaching and day-
time intellectual meandering. Once married to a woman—
Daisy—who offered him all the comforts of an honest
bourgeois housewife—"stability, symmetry, order, containment
were Daisy's strengths" (p. 126)—Herzog abandoned her in
favor of the wild and unfaithful Madeleine.

What actually happened? I gave up the shelter of an orderly,
purposeful, lawful existence because it bored me, and I felt it
was simply a slacker's life. (P. 103)

Madeleine, as well as being a Great Bitch, is also the great
architect of chaos in Herzog's life. She bounces checks, refuses

to clean up the house, and betrays Herzog with his best friend, Valentine Gersbach. Irresponsible and extravagant, she is everything that the dull Daisy is not. Does this make Herzog happy? Not on your life. " 'Jesus Christ,' " he cries as the checks come back " 'Can't you add! . . . We've got to have a little order in these surroundings.' " (p. 124). Divorce from Madeleine is as inevitable as was divorce from Daisy. Herzog can no more remain in their company than could Henderson in that of the Arnewi and the Wariri.

Herzog characterizes himself as a softy, a "naive" someone whose outlook on life is considered by most adults to be excessively childish, and he partly attributes the breakup of his second marriage to these aspects of his personality. Believing in "truth, friendship, devotion to children" (p. 266), and feeling that he is a man who has "tried to live out marvellous qualities vaguely comprehended" (p. 93), Herzog feels that his "innocent" beliefs and "childish" faith in the ultimate goodness of the world, are under attack from practically all his "adult" and "realistic" friends.

> *A very special sort of lunatic expects to inculcate his principles.* Sandor Himmelstein, Valentine Gersbach, Madeleine P. Herzog, Moses himself. *Reality Instructors.* They want to teach you—to punish you with—the lessons of the real. (P. 125)

Oddly, Herzog includes himself in this Augie March-type list of "imposers upon" (*The Adventures of Augie March,* p. 524), but the novel does not go far in consolidating Herzog's ironies at his own expense. If he is a "Reality Instructor," he is a benign version of the real thing, insisting for the most part that "realism" does not have to be "brutal" (p. 218), that "brotherhood is what makes a man human" (p. 272), and that " 'Man liveth not by Self alone, . . .' " (p. 272).

Herzog's Reality Instructors tend to take the opposite line. They are a hard-nosed lot who believe in "facts." As Sandor Himmelstein, Herzog's lawyer, tells Moses when his client begins to get a little abstract:

> ". . . Don't get highfalutin. I'm talking facts, not shit."
> "And you think a fact is what's nasty."
> "Facts *are* nasty."
> "You think they're true because they're nasty?"
> ". . . Don't give me that hoity-toity. I'm a Kike myself and

got my diploma in a stinking night school. Okay? Now let's both knock off this crap dreamy boy." (P. 86)

In the company of the "childish" Herzog, the Reality Instructors in addition to getting angry tend to get paternal and oddly sentimental. Sometimes it seems as if the presence of the "foolish" intellectual alone is enough to bring tears to a Reality Instructor's eyes. Herzog's innocence reminds them of their childhood and this breaks them up, while his "unreality" is so pathetic that it makes a grown man weep.

In one sense the Reality Instructors prove their own case. For, while Herzog goes around reasserting his faith in brotherhood, his "brothers"—Himmelstein; Dr. Edvig, the analyst; Gersbach—are busy giving Herzog some personal instruction in the art of deceit: Himmelstein passes his fees from Herzog on to Madeleine "*to buy clothing*" (p. 91); Edvig becomes fascinated with Herzog's "in session" descriptions of Madeleine, asks to meet her, and then, captivated, turns against his own patient; while Gersbach's long affair with Madeleine is conducted simultaneously to his holding best-friend status in Herzog's life.

Whose version of reality is the more convincing? The novel as a whole seems to side with the "Reality Instructors"—largely because Herzog's ideas are so forcefully contradicted by his experiences. However, the Reality Instructors are the usual bunch of hypocrites, liars, bitches and know-alls that surround a Bellow hero, and as such they create what we might call a "credibility gap." Moreover, while Herzog tends to categorize them in familiar terms as both "gold" and "shit," there seems, perhaps because a sexual betrayal is involved, to be more than the usual emphasis on the "shit." Madeleine, for example, for all her imperious manner, "masterful conduct" (p. 298), and perfect "Byzantine profile" (p. 298), is, Herzog tells us, "proud but not well-wiped" (p. 299), has a "dirty way" (p. 298) about her, and gives off unpleasant "odors of feminine secretions" (p. 298). Gersbach does not come off much better. He (and who is there to refute Herzog on this?) is a "charlatan, psychopath, with . . . hot phony eyes"[3] (p. 299).

By contrast, Herzog himself comes across as an insightful character—and he is the one with whom we identify and sympathize. Herzog, however, seems alone in his faith in humankind's potential for goodness. Or rather he finds himself in the company of one good man—his friend Lucas Asphalter. Asphalter is the one loyal and trustworthy character in the novel. It is Asphalter who first tells Herzog that he has been betrayed and Asphalter who is always ready to offer Herzog comfort in one form or another—a spare bed, a drink, a sympathetic ear. However, in the manner common to Bellow's characterizations of "good" men, Asphalter is more than passingly odd. A zoologist, Asphalter has become well known in scientific circles for trying to save his favorite monkey, Rocco,'s life by giving him mouth-to-mouth resuscitation. That Rocco was suffering from TB at the time has only added to the "scandal." Thus, on the melioristic side of things, we really have only Herzog to rely on.

Sometimes it seems as if Bellow, the hopeful optimist, through his mouthpiece Herzog, is doing battle with Bellow the novelist and his altogether less-compromising versions of reality. This kind of novelistic friction can produce astonishing results—one might think of Dostoevski's brilliant argument against his own beliefs in *The Brothers Karamazov*—but in *Herzog* the whole argument as to the true nature of reality (unlike the arguments of "The Grand Inquisitor") seems somehow peripheral to Bellow's larger concerns.

As the novel progresses, it becomes increasingly difficult to take Herzog seriously when he talks about "brotherhood." For he seems to make every effort to live in a self-enclosed world. Herzog's happiest times in the novel come at the end when he is holed up alone in his isolated, rundown country house in the Berkshires. When he scoops up a copy of Rozanov's *Solitaria* (Eugene Henderson's favorite game is solitaire), he seems the happiest man alive. And his happiness is only disturbed when his brother Will arrives and, behaving in a brotherly way, tries to convince Herzog to take a few days convalescence in a hospital (possibly a mental hospital). Herzog is quite happy to be terminally estranged from the world that he inhabits—a fact that calls into question the sincerity of his constant expressions of communal yearning and that undermines the supposedly humanistic vision that critics have discovered in so many Bellow novels.

Herzog's argument with the "Reality Instructors" ultimately comes to seem merely the expression of a much deeper Bellovian conflict: that between what Bellow conceives to be "childish" and "adult," and "feminine" and "male" principles in

American society. The reader comes away from *Herzog* with the feeling that Herzog is probably wrong about reality (it is not benign) and therefore correct in his assessments of what most Americans think it takes to be effectual, powerful, and manly in America. That is, the society's values create its own unpleasant reality. Herzog associatively aligns himself with all those whom American "male" realism has excluded from "public" life— most significantly women. However, Herzog is no feminist. He would like women to remain in the "private realm" (p. 94), and he would like men to set him free of it.

In an interview that he gave to *Life* magazine in 1970, Bellow described how writers of his generation

> suffer from the persistent American feeling that the intellectual life is somehow not virile. Artists and Professors like clergymen and librarians, are thought to be female. Our populist tradition requires the artist to represent himself as a man of the people and to conceal his real concern with thought. Maybe that's why we don't have more novels of ideas.[4]

Bellow goes on to suggest that "the powerful hold fiction writers in contempt" because they get no evidence from modern literature that anybody is thinking about significant questions. Seen in this light, *Herzog* seems not so much a defense of supposedly "feminine" and "childish" points of view, but an attempt to appease "the powerful" with big ideas and, paradoxically, to convince them that it is novels of ideas and not novels about fishing and hunting that are truly "manly." Bellow seems to be saying that Herzog and men like him may be intellectuals, but they are not sissies—give them half a chance and you'll discover them to be just as virile as your average businessman, politician, or Hemingway.

Most significantly, however, it seems to be exclusion from the male-dominated "public" world that plays such a big part in firing Herzog up intellectually: big ideas and "significant questions" are the payoff for accepting powerlessness.

Sometimes, indeed, *Herzog* seems to have been written almost as a textbook on sublimation. For (and perhaps this is why a book featuring comic arguments with Heidegger and Nietzsche could have remained on the *New York Times* best-seller list for so many months), at its deepest level the novel examines the therapeutic options available to a civilized man when his "sexual powers" have been "damaged" (p. 5) by a cheating wife and when unthinkable murder has leaped into his heart.

After his breakup with Madeleine, Herzog feels like "a convalescent" because he senses that he has lost the "ability to attract women" (p. 5). As a restorative he takes up with one of his night-school students—Ramona Donsella. Ramona is a "sexual professional (or priestess)," a "true sack artist" (p. 17) who keeps copies of Norman O. Brown's books on her bedside table. Ramona seems to specialize in sexual recuperation. She provides all the conventional preliminaries—wine, good food, exotic music—and her bedroom act includes black lace and lingerie and "spike-heeled shoes, three inches high" (p. 203) on which she makes her entrances.

Generally, "for the most high-minded reasons," Ramona carries on "like one of those broads in a girlie magazine" (p. 202). But this turns out to be all too much for Herzog. Ramona wants him "to go the whole hog" (p. 201), but Herzog does not want to turn himself into "a petit-bourgeois Dionysian" (p. 17). For Herzog, the erotic life, as directed by Ramona, represents a form of "liberation" that is all too extreme. He can neither restore himself nor get back at Madeleine by giving himself over to the "Mystical Body" (p. 202).

For a man in Herzog's position, from sex there is really nowhere to go but violence. Throughout the novel, Herzog sporadically imagines all kinds of pains and tortures for Madeleine and Gersbach. During one of his sessions of "self-analysis," he gives himself over to a fantasy of revenge.

> What if he had knocked her down, clutched her hair, dragged her screaming and fighting around the room, flogged her until her buttocks bled. What if he had! He should have torn her clothes, ripped off her necklace, brought his fists down on her head. (P. 10)

But the scenario ends with a whimper. "He rejected this mental violence, sighing. He was afraid he was really given in secret to this sort of brutality" (p. 10). Like Joseph in *Dangling Man*, Herzog does not "like to think what we are governed by" (*Dangling Man*, p. 83), and feeling that "his rage is so great and deep, so murderous, bloody, positively rapturous, that his arms and fingers ache to strangle them [Madeleine and Gersbach]," Herzog concludes that it is a good thing that the civilized forces of "social organization" (p. 220) exist to keep him in check.

It does indeed seem to be a good thing, when, two-thirds into the novel Herzog sets off from New York for Chicago with the intention of murdering Madeleine and Gersbach. Herzog's decision to take such drastic action is precipitated by an ugly scene that he witnesses in a New York courtroom.

Herzog is hanging around in the courts waiting to see his divorce lawyer, Simkin. Simkin is late, and Herzog wanders into a nearby courtroom. His attention is soon riveted by a gruesome case of child murder that is being tried. The background of the murderess is desperate. She is epileptic, crippled, poverty-stricken, and had been sexually abused as a child. Her lover, indifferent and senseless, watched while she battered her child to death. Herzog is sickened by what he hears, doubly so, for the trial has a personal significance for him that is not immediately apparent. Early in the novel, Herzog has learned that Madeleine and Gersbach have locked his daughter, Junie, in their car; apparently so that they could get on with a lover's tiff in peace. The child murder thus recalls for Herzog the cruelty to his own child. For the reader, and presumably for Herzog's unconscious, there are even more points of reference. The mother of the murdered child is a "redheaded woman" with a "ruddy face" (p. 235), something that recalls Valentine Gersbach's flaming red hair. She also wears an orthopedic boot, reinforcing the association with Gersbach, who has only one good leg. Of the witnesses for the prosecution, one is a "salesman in the storm-window business" (p. 237). Our association must be with Herzog erecting storm windows in his backyard immediately prior to Madeleine's dismissing him from their house. The triangle of Herzog's personal drama is thus exaggerated and repeated in the courtroom. The defendants are, projectively, Madeleine and Gersbach; the prosecuting witness, Herzog himself.

When he gets to Chicago, Herzog retrieves his father's old handgun from his stepmother's apartment and rushes off to do away with his betrayers. However, when he arrives at his old house, Herzog first sights Gersbach through a window, tenderly bathing little Junie. To his own astonishment, he is moved rather than incensed. When his daughter is safely out of the bathroom, Herzog has a chance to fire but he merely turns away.

There were two bullets in the chamber. . . . But they would stay there. Herzog clearly recognized that. Very softly he stepped down from his perch. . . . He saw his child in the kitchen, looking up at Mady . . . and he edged through the gate into the alley. Firing this pistol was nothing but a thought. (P. 257)

For Herzog, violence is no more the way to quiet his inner rage than is wild sexual activity the way to restore his sexual powers.

What can this civilized Herzog do to help resolve his crisis? He can, and does, "change it all into language" (p. 272). Language is Herzog's abundant compensation. In a central passage in the novel, Herzog attempts to explain to his friend Lucas Asphalter just why he has been expending so much energy on writing mental letters.

Still, what can thoughtful people and humanists do but struggle toward suitable words? Take me, for instance. I've been writing letters helter-skelter in all directions. More words. I go after reality with language. Perhaps I'd like to change it all into language, to force Madeleine and Gersbach to have a *Conscience*. There's a word for you. I must be trying to keep tight the tensions without which human beings can no longer be called human. If they don't suffer they've gotten away from me. And I've filled the world with letters to prevent their escape. I want them in human form, and so I conjure up a whole environment and catch them in the middle. I put my whole heart into these constructions. But they are constructions. (P. 272)

Madeleine and Gersbach changed into language become altogether more manageable. Herzog does not say so, but it seems as if finding "suitable words" to describe his situation does much more to restore his potency than either Ramona's nightclub act or his fooling around with guns. Herzog's manic correspondence with all and sundry is both an expression of his deepest frustrations and an antidote to his suffering.

Unlike the heroes who precede him, Herzog does not "agonize" so much as use his agony to light wonderful intellectual fires; fires that lend an aura of brilliance to the novel. But, almost perversely, we know that a Herzog restored to full "health" will also be a less vitally intellectual Herzog. The novel, in fact, must end when Herzog is "released" from his obsession with Madeleine, for he is bound to be simultaneously released from his need to "fill the world with letters." And, indeed, when Herzog does finally, joyously, feel that his "servitude" to

Madeleine is over, that his heart is "released from its grisly heaviness and frustration" (p. 313), he soon discovers that he has no further need to engage in intellectual conflicts with philosophers, writers, and politicians.

At the end of the novel, Herzog repairs to his country house in Ludeyville—a parodic Romantic retreat, a Yeatsian tower that Herzog ironically refers to as "Herzog's Folly." Here he wanders around his twenty acres of hillside and woodlot, moving closer and closer toward the deep internal silence that he has been longing for. Finally, alone in his garden, feeling *"satisfied to be, to be just as it is willed, and for as long as [he] may remain in occupancy"* (p. 340), Herzog discovers that he has "no messages for anyone. Nothing. Not a single word" (p. 341).

In Bellow's early novels, we remain mired in the problems of heroes who are caught between a desire for order and a fear of limitation, and who seem inordinately pained by their need to repress their sexual and aggressive instincts. But in *Herzog,* Bellow allows his hero to take off from these problems: they are the rocket fuel but they do not determine where the rocket will go. From *Herzog* onward, thanks to their ability to change reality into language—or any kind of sophisticated internal musing—Bellow's heroes no longer struggle with the fact that they are being paralyzed, bullied, cheated, repressed, oppressed, or in some vital way restricted either by an individual, a group of individuals, or society as a whole. Instead they seem almost grateful to find themselves in the state of being that they know catapults them into higher states of mind. Bellow's "late" heroes give up on trying to solve the insoluble problems of their existence. However, when the troubled Bellovian hero is no longer really troubled, the reader tends to sit back and watch the intellectual show. It is a wonderful show, but its effect is to distance rather than engage us with the novel.

8

Mr. Sammler's Planet

For Artur Sammler, New York at the end of the sixties has got "out of hand" (p. 34). A septuagenarian, a man who has survived the worst that Nazi murderers and Polish anti-Semites had to throw at him, Sammler is now living another nightmare. In Manhattan, "Dark romanticism" has taken hold:

> The sexual ways of the seraglio and of the Congo bush adopted by the emancipated masses of New York . . . the right to be uninhibited, spontaneous, urinating, defecating, belching, coupling in all positions, tripling, quadrupling, polymorphous, noble in being primitive. . . . The dreams of the nineteenth century poets polluted the psychic atmosphere of the great boroughs and suburbs of New York. (P. 32)

Sammler has known London in prewar Bloomsbury days, halcyon days of civilized discussion with acquaintances such as H. G. Wells, and he has known Auschwitz, where his wife was murdered and he climbed out of a mass grave, one eye lost to a Nazi rifle butt. He is a man who knows the difference between civilization and chaos and he has plenty to say about the "free ways of barbarism" that contemporary New Yorkers are presently indulging in beneath an umbrella of "civilized order, property rights [and] refined technological organization" (p. 7). Sammler feels that with just a little more barbarism the protective umbrella may disappear altogether.

Until very recently, *Mr. Sammler's Planet* has largely been read as an aberration in Bellow's canon: "a work of social indignation, a radical revolt against the radical revolt of 1968."[1] Some critics, especially those who had devoted articles or books to explaining and admiring Bellow as a "life-affirming" writer, felt almost betrayed by Artur Sammler's book-length harangue against radical students, libidinous young women, and mem-

143

bers of the black underclass. John Jay Clayton, in a postscript to his book, *Saul Bellow: In Defense of Man,* was incensed enough to compare Saul Bellow to "Spiro Agnew and George Wallace." His book, scheduled to end with the sentence "It is his [Bellow's] sympathy with . . . manifold humanity, the apprehension of the mystery inherent in living human beings—a mystery which signifies their value—for which we read Saul Bellow," had to be rescheduled because of the anomalous Mr. Sammler. The postscript concludes on a more tentative note "I hope . . . that Bellow returns to the planet he used to share with us."[2]

For Max Schulz "the impoverished view of man [that] Bellow gives us in *Mr. Sammler's Planet*" seems to reflect either "a real shifting of philosophical ground" on Bellow's part or a "fictionally undigested reaction to the frustrations of mid-twentieth century existence."[3] Such it would seem are the dangers of fooling with a living novelist.

Bellow's responses to the upheavals of the late 1960s are well known and when Artur Sammler is championing order, sexual conservatism, public restraint, and self-control, he does indeed seem to be little more than a mouthpiece for his creator. As Ben Siegel has pointed out, while novelists do not necessarily share their hero's views, "Artur Sammler's reactions to people and events are totally consistent with those expressed by Saul Bellow in . . . essay, lecture and interview."[4] For the most part, Sammler expresses Bellow's disgust with the degenerated world in which he felt himself to be living fifteen years ago. However, Bellow the novelist, as I have noted elsewhere (see previous chapter), is governed by creative impulses that do not always square with the presentation of a one-sided view of things—whatever that side may be. And, while Sammler's pontifications lend the novel its reactionary air, Bellow's fictional methodology ensures that Sammler will turn out to be as twisted a spokesman for "order" as was Augie March for "freedom."

Artur Sammler puts a lot of energy into vilifying the world in which he lives (the Western world), the city that he inhabits (New York), and the people who surround him (New Yorkers), but, not unpredictably, he turns out to be strangely and powerfully drawn to the world that he is inclined to renounce, the social system that he is inclined to mistrust, and characters whom he is inclined to fear or disapprove of. For, while Sammler flirts with the transcendent and claims that he wants "with

God, to be free from the bondage of the ordinary and the finite[,] a soul released from Nature, from impressions and everyday life. . . ." (p. 117), some other part of his being—a part that he fights—always finds itself "persuasively drawn back to human conditions" (p. 118).

Similarly, Sammler, as a witness to the decadence of contemporary New York, the libidinous excesses of the sixties and the radical breakdown of certain civilized moral codes, champions efficient policing and personal restraint. Yet, as a survivor of the Nazi holocaust, Sammler remains more than a little suspicious of arbitrary order, extensive organization, and rigid limits on individual liberty. Finally, the bookish, withdrawn Sammler, who has determined to live out the last years of his life poring over Meister Eckhardt and the Bible in some drear basement of the New York Public Library, "inexplicably" and "against his own stable principles" (p. 11) finds himself compulsively drawn to observe the activities of a criminal: a black pickpocket who as the novel progresses Sammler comes both to sympathize with and to admire.

More ruthlessly than any of Bellow's other heroes, Sammler embodies the contradictions involved in pursuing a Bellovian life on earth. As Sammler himself puts it, if the individual can achieve no ascetic or transcendent triumph, he is destined to confront a series of impossible choices; let him but once come firmly to rest and he is doomed to adopt or recognize the farcical aspects of his position.

> Once take a stand, once draw a baseline, and contraries will assail you. Declare for normalcy and you will be stormed by aberrancies. All postures are mocked by their opposites. This is what happens when the individual begins to be drawn back from disinterestedness to creaturely conditions. (P. 118)

Interestingly, the social and historical background of *Mr. Sammler's Planet* seems to have been almost tailor-made to suit Bellow's fictional preoccupations. In *Henderson the Rain King,* Bellow designed a world to express a fixed set of ideational contradictions. In *Mr. Sammler's Planet,* rather than having to resort to the creation of an "imaginary" place in order to be able schematically to control his material, Bellow was able to superimpose a set of fixed ideas without, overtly, having to upset the sense of conveyed reality. In a way, what Bellow makes use of are "found metaphors"; the historical actualities of the late sixties—the "boundary breaking" moonshot, the radical conflict of police and students or police and criminals— lend themselves to the kind of schematic polarization to which Bellow is attracted.

It is precisely because the events in the novel are real historical events that *Mr. Sammler's Planet* is so revealing. Mr. Sammler's New York throws up a world of contradictions similar in almost every way to that of the Arnewi and the Wariri in *Henderson the Rain King*. But, we do not get "a fix" on Henderson in the same way as on Sammler because, on the surface anyway, Henderson "dangles" between bizarre and exotic modes of tribal behavior. Henderson is caught between arbitrary rituals of limit and mysterious magical liberations, between a world of bovine stupidity (the Arnewi) and one founded on death and violence (the Wariri). Sammler is caught between the indifferent, dull-witted police and the radical students, between the oppressive white man and the violent and angry black man.

Moreover, and most important, the major difference between Sammler and Henderson—and indeed, all Bellow's other heroes—is that where the other heroes seem either directly or at the metaphoric level to be suspicious of, scared of, or in conflict with the "dark" side of their personalties—what Sammler calls the "black" side, the "child, black, redskin" (p. 162) and we might add "female" parts of the self—Sammler, while he remains a "split" personality, seems more vitally alarmed by actual black people, actual "redskins," and actual women. In *Mr. Sammler's Planet,* that part of Bellow's hero's character that fears "chaos" comes out in what some might say are its true colors as misogyny and racism.

Those critics and readers who felt betrayed by *Mr. Sammler's Planet* felt that way because Manhattan in 1969 and not Chicago in 1930 *(The Adventures of Augie March)* or an Africa beyond both geography and history *(Henderson the Rain King)* was the novel's setting. As a result, the external struggle between civilization and barbarism, order and chaos, took place not in some distant region of the imagination but on Broadway and its environs. For the women, blacks, and academic liberals who, perhaps for years, had been buying Bellow's books and reading them with pleasure there was a sudden insight that when Bellow wrote about characters who "communicate[d] chaos" (p. 67), he meant them!

The force of this realization perhaps also blinded readers to the fact that if Sammler disliked students, he also hated the police; that while he was "not against civilization, nor against politics, institutions, nor against order" (p. 277), he sympathized with the youthful desire to attack "a corrupt tradition built on neurosis and falsehood" (p. 36). Moreover, Sammler constantly bears in mind that "no politics, no order" (p. 277) intervened to prevent his wife and himself from being murderously dumped into a mass grave by the Nazis.

These divergent tendencies in Sammler's personality do tend to be obscured by Sammler's vituperative intermezzos on females: "[They] were naturally more prone to grossness, had more smells, needed more washing, clipping, binding, pruning, grooming, perfuming and training" (p. 36); students: "[h]airy, dirty, without style, levellers, ignorant" (p. 36); and all the millions of civilized people who have "acquired the peculiar aim of sexual niggerhood for everyone" (p. 162). Nevertheless, as Sammler's relationship with the black pickpocket profoundly reveals, the divergent tendencies are there.

Theoretically Sammler is in a blue funk about crime. In New York City, law and order has broken down. Signs of vandalism are everywhere visible (telephone kiosks smashed and used as urinals), and they only bespeak a greater disintegration. On the uptown bus that he regularly takes home from the library, Sammler has noticed a pickpocket at work. He has informed the police—the police are not interested. Sammler continues to observe the pickpocket and although he doesn't want to acknowledge it, he begins to experience a *frisson* everytime he catches the criminal in action. Claiming that he doesn't "give a damn for the glamour, the style, the art of criminals" (p. 10), Sammler yet subscribes to the Romantic notion that "in evil as in art there was illumination" (p. 11) and, by the end of the novel he has come around to describing the pickpocket as embodying "a certain princeliness . . . a mad spirit. But mad with an idea of *noblesse*" (p. 294).

Watching the pickpocket at work, Sammler reserves most of his anger for the man's victims—"Zero instincts, no grasp of New York" (p. 10)—and, perhaps most significantly, Sammler is aware that "he . . . received from the crime the benefit of enlarged vision" (p. 11). Like all Bellow's heroes, Sammler finds that crisis and danger are potent catalysts, able to heighten perception and grant rare moments of almost hallucinatory

vision. Sammler is not the contented scholarly bibliophile that
he claims to be and, in a familiar way, he courts disaster when a
more orderly life could be his for the taking.

> He saw a crime committed. He reported it to the cops. . . . He
> might then have stayed away from that particular bus, but
> instead he tried to repeat the experience. . . .
> . . . It was a powerful event, and illicitly—that is against his
> own stable principles—he craved a repetition. (Pp. 9–11)

In essence, Sammler's behavior is no different from Henderson's when he moves from the Arnewi to the Wariri or Herzog's
when he transfers his affections from Daisy to Madeleine. Sammler cannot stay in the library and take a different bus home
because he is powerfully drawn to danger—to the "chaotic."

Animal-like, primitive, sexual, and violent, the pickpocket at
first appears to be the living opposite of the civilized, dry, and
withdrawn Sammler. However, Bellow subtly sets up an identity
between the two characters: both Sammler and the pickpocket
wear dark glasses though neither is blind, both men (as the
reader is finally made aware) are victims—Sammler has experi-
enced Nazi brutality at its worst, while, toward the end of the
novel, the pickpocket is almost beaten to death by Sammler's
violent son-in-law, Eisen; both are interested in stylish clothes
and, perhaps of equal importance, both men apparently have
large penises.

The suggestion that the black pickpocket is Sammler's palpable "double" (an inarticulate Allbee or Dahfu) is reinforced
in a moment of profound theatricality. The pickpocket, aware
that Sammler has been observing him, follows the old man
home and catches up with him in the lobby of his apartment
building. Instead of assaulting Sammler, the pickpocket traps
Sammler against a wall, unzips his fly, and directs Sammler to
look downward. A primitive but powerful warning to stop his
observations of the pickpocket at work, Sammler is quick to get
the black man's message. The pickpocket departs, never having
uttered a word and Sammler returns to his room. As he recup-
erates, Sammler is moved to an interesting meditation.

> Sammler was again thinking of the pickpocket . . . the two
> pairs of dark glasses, the lizard thick curving tube in the
> hand. . . . Ugly, odious; laughable, but nevertheless impor-
> tant. . . . Of course he and the pickpocket were different. . . .

Their mental, characterological, spiritual profiles were miles apart. In the past, Mr. Sammler had thought that in this same biological respect he was comely enough, in his own Jewish way. (Pp. 65–66)

The stress of difference, almost arbitrary at this point in the novel, has the overall effect of suggesting sameness. When he describes the pickpocket and himself as inhabiting "adjoining regions of recklessness" (p. 6), Sammler comes close to acknowledging the pickpocket's relevance for him as an alter ego.

Sammler, like all Bellow's heroes is a combination of two selves. Interestingly, like Joseph in *Dangling Man*, Sammler divides his personality into an "earlier" self and a "later" self. The "earlier" self is reckless, while the "later" self treads more carefully.

It was the earlier Sammler, the Sammler of London and Cracow, who had gotten off the bus at Columbus Circle foolishly eager to catch sight of a black criminal. He now had to avoid the bus, dreading another encounter. He had been warned, positively instructed to appear no more. (Pp. 118–19)

Like Joseph's two selves, Sammler's "earlier" and "later" selves coexist in a single present self. The dominant "self" appears to be the "later" self, but Sammler is always forced to wrestle with the curious, adventurous side of his personality.

While Sammler is engaged with the pickpocket, and with the pulls and tugs of his "earlier" self, he is simultaneously engaged with a matter that strains and reveals the resources of his "later" self. Sammler's nephew, Elya Gruner, lies critically ill in a Manhattan hospital. He has suffered an aneuryism of the brain and only has days to live. For Sammler, Gruner is a model of restraint and dependability. A retired doctor, a man who has "done his duty" (p. 83), Gruner appears to uphold all the values that Sammler respects—values that Sammler feels are evanescent at the present time. The father of two ingrate children, Wallace and Angela, Gruner has extended his familial responsibilities to cover Sammler and Sammler's crazy daughter Shula/Slawa, plucking them out of a DP camp after the war and setting them up in New York.

Gruner is a representative man for Sammler, "devoted to ideas of conduct which seem discredited" (p. 261), he represents both a dying civilization and perhaps more significantly, the part of Sammler that is drawn to order, limitation, and a quiet life. As Sammler tells Gruner's daughter Angela, Gruner has achieved a level of "goodness" that Sammler himself (for reasons that the reader is aware of) has failed to attain.

> Your father had his assignments. Husband, medical man—he was a good doctor, family man, success. . . . We have our assignments. Feeling, outgoingness, expressiveness, kindness, heart—all these fine human things which by a peculiar turn of opinion strike people now as shady activities. Openness and candour about vices seem far easier. Anyway, there is Elya's assignment. That's what's in his good face. That's why he has such a human look. . . . He had an unsure loyalty to certain pure states. He knew there had been good men before him, that there were good men to come, and he wanted to be one of them. I think he did all right. I don't come out nearly so well myself. (P. 303)

Highly conscious, extraordinarily perceptive, spiritually inclined and yet adventurous, Sammler is drawn to affirm the value of an ordinary, dull, dutiful, materialistic character like Gruner. For Sammler, Gruner and the pickpocket are symbolic forces in the larger battle that society has engaged between the forces of civilization and those of chaos. Problematically, as far as Sammler is concerned, Gruner adheres to a set of values that Sammler respects and subscribes to but that he himself often contradicts in his behavior; to make matters worse, the pickpocket "breaks boundaries" in a way that enthralls Sammler as much as it horrifies him. Sammler is caught between the devil and the deep blue sea, between the sins of the pickpocket and the virtues of Gruner, between the values of civilization and those of its rebellious opponents.

However, if Sammler has a tendency to rigidly divide the world into good and bad parts, Bellow is at pains to more thoroughly demonstrate how *all* postures are mocked by their opposites. On the surface, symbolic extensions of Sammler's own internal conflicts, Gruner and the pickpocket are not, however, the clear and defined "polarities" that they at first appear to be. For, while on one level the pickpocket and Gruner extend Sammler's inner conflict, on another level they more accurately reproduce it. Gruner, it transpires, has throughout his long career as a gynecologist, "performed abortions to oblige old

Mafia friends" (p. 162), and just as the pickpocket is transformed from an oppressor into a victim and, thereby, into a
sympathetic character, so too is Gruner revealed to be the opposite of what he seems. For the reader, the paradox is clear, but
Sammler resists such awkward "characterological" complications. Unwilling to admit his attraction to the pickpocket
(pp. 10–11), he is equally reluctant to contemplate the import
of Gruner's criminal activity (p. 162). Whenever Sammler's
careful divisions into good and bad are threatened, he is
obliged to overlook or dismiss the disturbing factors.

Bellow characterizes Sammler as a "dangling man" drawn to
both order and to chaos, and Sammler is recognizably a member of Bellow's family of heroes. But, the pickpocket and
Gruner are also, in a sense, "dangling men" for, as in all the
novels, they are minor characters who embody contradictory
characteristics themselves: Gruner swings between a world of
crime and one that is more orderly and conventional, while the
pickpocket is both a petty criminal and a more gracious, "aristocratic" personality. In Bellow's conflict-ridden world, there are
few, if any, characters who are what they at first appear to be.

Interestingly, Sammler associates himself with Gruner in a
way that complements and reverses the manner of his disassoci-
ation from the pickpocket. Having told Angela Gruner that "on
the surface I don't have much in common with Elya" (p. 302),
Sammler goes on to explain that on a more profound level he
and Gruner share "an unsure loyalty to certain pure states"
(p. 303). Sammler would like to deny the validity of his "earlier," "surface," adventurous self and emphasize the profound
"civilized" aspects of his being. On his own prejudiced terms,
Sammler is right to disassociate himself from the pickpocket
and line up alongside Gruner. But unable to act in the way that
he insists Gruner behaves, and equally incapable of emulating
the pickpocket, Sammler remains "dangling" between them.

Flanked by the pickpocket and Gruner, Sammler feels that he
moves through a society that is, both literally and metaphorically, enacting a struggle between black and white sides. From
everything that Sammler sees about him, "black" seems to be
winning. Even Sammler's eccentric daughter Shula/Slawa (she
is a Jewish Catholic with a Hebrew-Polish name who fills her
appartment with items culled from New York's trash baskets)
has not escaped the "psychic pollution." Shula/Slawa believes
that her father is writing a memoir of H. G. Wells and in order

to help his (wholly imaginary) research, she steals a manuscript, "The Future of the Moon," from Dr. Govinda Lal, an Indian scientist who is guest-lecturing at Columbia. In Shula/Slawa's petty crime, Sammler discovers a representative malaise.

> But even Shula, though a scavenger or magpie, had never stolen before. Then suddenly she too was like the negro pickpocket. From the black side, strong currents were sweeping over everyone. Child, black, redskin,—the unspoiled Seminole against the horrible Whiteman. Millions of civilized people wanted oceanic, boundless, primitive, neckfree nobility, experienced a strange release of galloping impulses. . . . (Pp. 161–62)

Sammler, of course, is loathe to acknowledge that he himself is occasionally the victim of "galloping impulses" (the pickpocket obsession), and in his own way enacts, at the psychological level, a quite unmistakeable black/white struggle.

On the macrocosmic or cosmic level, it is Sammler's reaction to the Apollo 11 moon shot and to Dr. Lal's book on human colonization of the moon that reveal the nature of his "dangling." Sammler responds to the moon shot in precisely the opposite way that Norman Mailer does in *Of a Fire on the Moon.* For Sammler, space travel is not so much an instance of man reducing space, setting fresh boundaries, penetrating mystery, and replacing God with Technology, it is rather yet another manifestation of the unrepressed contemporary push toward the illimitable. When Wallace Gruner asks Sammler if, given the opportunity, he would go to the moon Sammler replies:

> To the moon? But I don't even want to go to Europe, and. . . . Besides, if I had my choice, I'd prefer the ocean bottom. In Dr. Piccard's bathysphere. I seem to be a depth man rather than a height man. I do not personally care for the illimitable. The ocean, however deep, has a top and bottom, whereas there is no sky ceiling. (Pp. 183–84)

Sammler wants limits—tops and bottoms—and rockets are an attempt to break free. They come, we might say, from "the black side."

On the other hand, the "infinite" is appealing to Sammler. He already feels that he has "gaps" in his substance (p. 43), and he regards the earth with what he thinks of as "farewell-detachment . . . earth-departure-objectivity" (p. 134). However,

Sammler does not think that the moon shot and subsequent life on the moon are "the way to get out of spatial-temporal prison" (p. 53). What Sammler actually wants is beautifully expressed in his desire to go to the ocean bottom. He wants to achieve the infinite not by dying (who does?) but through a transcendence in life. He would like the world he lives in, in all aspects of it, to be ordered, enclosed, "limited," but he would like simultaneously to be out of that world. On the seabed, Sammler would be "weightless" but within "limits"; the moon, in a more frightening manner, offers weightlessness (the infinite) and the illimitable.

Sammler's desire to "transcend" is the thematic counterpoint to his engagement with the world of "sex-excrement militancy" (p. 43). The closest he gets to "transcendence" is to exhibit an almost postmortem detachment from his own experiences. In this respect he extends the push towards "transcendence" that Bellow began in *Herzog* and that culminates in Charlie Citrine's obsession with the theosophy of Rudolf Steiner. It should be clear that by "transcendence" I do not wish to invoke Emerson et al, but to refer to Bellow's late heroes attempts to achieve a certain remoteness from their own lives: they, in fact, aspire to a condition where all feeling can be neutralized, anesthetized, and turned to spectral "ideas" or better. Herzog "changes it all into language," Sammler changes it all into "ideas," and Citrine, as we shall see, has received the "light-in-being" (*Humboldt's Gift*, p. 177).

If Sammler likes to entertain himself by "considering the earth not as a stone cast but as something to cast oneself from— to be divested of" (p. 51), Bellow has given him the perfect opportunity to do so. For, unlike Bellow's other heroes, Sammler is released by age and inclination from the world of sexual wrangling; free of the desire to either "know who he is" or "change his life"; free of money problems—he is supported by the philanthropic Gruner—and, for the most part he is burdened with only a minimum of familial responsibility. It is no wonder that Sammler feels himself to be a "visiting consciousness" (p. 73) who is "very nearly out of it" (p. 134). For in Bellow's novels, not to have trouble with women and money does not leave you very much to do. Sammler is both set apart and disembodied by Bellow:

Mr. Sammler did feel somewhat separated from the rest of his species, if not in some fashion severed—severed not so

much by age as by preoccupations too different and remote,
disproportionate on the side of the spiritual, Platonic, Augus-
tinian, thirteenth century. As the traffic poured, the wind
poured, the sun . . . shining and pouring through openings
in his substance, through his gaps. As if he has been cast by
Henry Moore. With holes, lacunae. (P. 43)

In this ghostly state, Sammler should no doubt be able to see
things about as clearly as they can be seen. To this effect the
tendency of Sammler's personality, even more than that of
Herzog's, is to intellectualize his experience into abstraction
and distance it through generalization. The effect though, on
the novel overall (as many have noted) is to turn large sections
of *Mr. Sammler's Planet* into tedious stretches of what appears to
be extremely dry "philosophy."[5] However, in order to understand the novel in its broadest terms—that is as a Bellow novel
and not a Bellow tract—it is important not to isolate the content
of Sammler's monologues from that of Sammler's behavior and
from other contradictory feelings that he expresses.

Sammler largely derives his pessimism about contemporary
society (and thereby his yearning to transcend it) both induc-
tively—through his observation of friends, relatives, and acquaintances whom he says "communicate chaos" (p. 67)—and
directly from his own unpleasant experiences on the streets of
Manhattan. For the characters in his immediate circle, Sammler
feels that he is a "registrar of madness" (p. 118). Bruch, a distant relative tells Sammler that he masturbates behind his brief-
case at the sight of fleshy Puerto Rican women's arms; Feffer, a
young acquaintance reports his "indiscriminate bedroom adventures" (p. 67); and Angela Gruner comes to confide her own
polymorphous sexual perversities.

When Sammler steps out, things are even worse. First there is
his bizarre mugging at the hands of the pickpocket, and then
Sammler is shouted down by a Philistine student who is in the
audience at Columbia where he is guest-lecturing on Tawney,
Orwell, and Wells ("Why do you listen to this effete old shit?
What has he got to tell you? His balls are dry. He's dead. He
can't come" [p. 42]). From all this Sammler concludes that New
York is a place where "you could see the suicidal impulses of
civilization pushing strongly" (p. 33). And, given his experiences, this does not seem unreasonable. However, almost perversely, Sammler only seems genuinely troubled by his experi-

ences *after* he has transformed them into a set of general ideas. It is what people "symbolize" rather than what they are that upsets Sammler's equilibrium. For, while Sammler is disgusted by the world that his friends' and relatives' "weaknesses" represent, he is not disgusted by the characters themselves. Sammler excuses Bruch because, like himself he has been a victim of the Nazis. Feffer is one of Sammler's more valued acquaintances, and, about Angela Gruner, Sammler announces that he feels "no prejudice about perversion, about sexual matters" (p. 296). In its "particularized" form, the outside world is equally benign; the pickpocket, as we have seen, Sammler comes to regard as a "prince." Only the students remain as horrible in the flesh as in the mind.

It is perhaps for this reason—Sammler's ability to detach what characters symbolize from what they are—that Sammler is able, at the end of the novel, to perform an astonishing about-face and come up with a typically Bellovain "affirmation" of the world and its inhabitants. Ostensibly, Sammler's "affirmations" are inspired by Elya Gruner. In the old Mafia doctor's Rolls Royce, Sammler is being driven to visit Gruner for what is probably to be the last time. As Sammler and Gruner's chauffeur Emil cruise through Manhattan, Sammler peers through the window to observe "the subculture of the underprivileged" (p. 280). "By a convergence of all minds and all movements the conviction transmitted by this crowd [on the street] seemed to be that reality was a terrible thing, and that the final truth about mankind was overwhelming and crushing" (p. 280). Whether it is thoughts of Gruner—the one good man that Sammler knows—or just a thought out of the blue, Sammler is suddenly urged to reject this "vulgar, cowardly conclusion . . . with all his heart" (p. 280). When Sammler arrives at the hospital, Gruner is already dead. Sammler insists on going to view Elya's body in the morgue. Once there, he stares at his nephew's face and intones a mental prayer that seems to reiterate the "affirmative" frame of mind that he is in. Gruner has done "what was required of him," he has been "much kinder" than Sammler himself could ever be. Most importantly,

he was aware that he must meet, and he did meet—through all the confusion and degraded clowning of this life through which we are speeding—he did meet the terms of his contract. The terms which in his inmost heart, each man knows.

As I know mine. As all know. For that is the truth of it—that we all know, God, that we know, that we know, we know, we know. (P. 313)

This ending, like so many of Bellow's endings, is extremely moving and has a profound lyric intensity. However, a reader unfamiliar with Bellow's novels might, at this point, be forgiven for thinking that he was going crazy. Hasn't this character, Sammler, just spent almost three hundred pages outlining how there is something terminally rotten in the state of New York? Hasn't he sniffed out the "psychic" pollution, trod the dog-fouled pathways, and felt himself surrounded by perverts and criminals? Where are these last-page affirmations coming from? Familiar readers must have felt gypped, not confused. This was one novel where Bellow had no right to start letting his hero "affirm." This wasn't Bellow's world we had here but some horrible, mean-spirited, reactionary negative version of it.

Or is it? Sammler's world is really not too different from the one inhabited by all Bellow's heroes. Most of Bellow's heroes are surrounded by cheats, liars, betrayers, characters who steal their money, characters who steal their wives, wives who steal their money, and so on. Sammler has to contend with a mugger, a rude student, and a whole society that seems to have given itself over to Dionysian excesses. However, Sammler's cardinal sin is to do what a Bellow hero is never supposed to do— express hate for a Bellovian world that is clearly hateful. Sammler's last-minute affirmations are thus characterologically shocking—but they are no less groundless than those of his forebears.

9
Humboldt's Gift

The central figure in *Humboldt's Gift* is not the eponymous Von Humboldt Fleisher but a character called Charlie Citrine. Given Bellow's propensity to title his novels after their heroes— *The Adventures of Augie March, Henderson the Rain King, Herzog, Mr. Sammler's Planet*—we might expect to find Humboldt at the center of things. The misleading title, however, leads to a central issue in Bellow's fiction. For, having gradually removed his novels' heroes into a state of almost postmortem detachment, Bellow, in *Humboldt's Gift,* makes a brief attempt to set a more substantial (and less autobiographical) figure in the foreground. For thirty pages or so it seems as if Humboldt, a manic, brilliant, self-destructive poet, is going to dominate the novel. However, neither Bellow nor his narrator Citrine can sustain an interest in portraying Von Humboldt Fleisher and *Humboldt's Gift* soon disintegrates into *The Adventures of Charlie Citrine,* a novel featuring a more familiar Bellovian protagonist.

Bellow's failure to get inside the character of the driven and tormented Fleisher should not really surprise us.[1] Throughout his canon, an ambivalence about the self-image of modern self-destructive, parodically Romantic artists has manifested itself both discursively and in Bellow's unwillingness to make an artist of his heroes. The energy of Bellow's own obsession—the fate of a man "paralyzed" by the need to make a series of impossible choices—forcefully leads Bellow away from his half-hearted attempt to conjure Fleisher and back to the territory he knows so well—the character of a "dangling man"—ineluctably the subject matter of *Humboldt's Gift.*

"I am compelled to repeat" (p. 112), Charlie Citrine remarks by way of explaining his sporadic reiteration of a certain event throughout the novel, but, in its full weight, this short phrase is a suitable epigraph to *Humboldt's Gift* and perhaps to Bellow's entire canon. What is repeated in *Humboldt's Gift* (more intensely than Citrine's haunting memory of the destitute Fleisher eating a pretzel stick by a Manhattan curbside)[2] is the dominant pattern of Bellow's fiction.

A historian/biographer-cum-playwright who is "making . . . claims to order, rationality [and] prudence" (p. 378), Citrine, like Sammler and Augie before him, becomes unnecessarily entangled with a violent if comical underworld figure—Rinaldo Cantabile. Seriously engaged with the theosophy of Dr. Rudolf Steiner, and fascinated by the possibilities of the soul's transcending the body, Citrine, like Herzog, nevertheless involves himself in a complex and time-consuming love affair that is apparently centered on the erotic. However, in *Humboldt's Gift,* Citrine's common Bellovian dilemma—searching for "order," he behaves in such a way as to make its achievement impossible—is most significantly revealed through a schematic separation of his inner and outer worlds.

In *Augie March,* "order" is represented by Augie's dream of living in a house in the countryside surrounded by an adored and adoring extended family; similarly, for Tommy Wilhelm in *Seize the Day,* his Roxbury garden, in his imagination, represents peace and tranquility; even Moses Herzog tends to conceive of external order as a necessary accompaniment to internal order. Charlie Citrine goes a step further. For Citrine, the inner world itself, the world inside his head, is both Augie and Wilhelm's garden of delight. Citrine's concept of "order" is an almost ineffable element in his being, an autonomous part of his Self that exists independently of any relation to the "outside" world.

> I want it to be clear however, that I speak as a person who had lately received or experienced light. I don't mean "The light." I mean a kind of light-in-the-being, a thing difficult to be precise about, especially in an account like this, where so many cantankerous erroneous silly and delusive objects, actions and phenomena are in the foreground. (P. 177)

In *Humboldt's Gift,* the "background" and "foreground" of Citrine's narrative correspond to his inner and outer worlds. The split is decisive and metaphorically represents worlds of order and chaos. Citrine is in an advanced Bellovian stage, in which the putting of his life in order has nothing to do with working out his feelings about his ex-wife Denise, deciding whether or not to marry his lover Renata, finding financial equilibrium, setting up a stable home, or even coming to terms with his own neuroses. Discovering the-light-in-being has put him beyond all that fiddle.

What is interesting is that Citrine's "light," if it can be elucidated, is vitally connected to childhood. What Citrine has recaptured is a Wordsworthian innocence. Having forgotten how to trail clouds of glory for five decades, he has now redis-covered the ability.

> In the first decade of life I knew this light and even knew how to breathe it in. But this early talent or gift or inspiration, given up for the sake of maturity or realism (practicality, self-preservation, the fight for survival) was now edging back. (Pp. 177–78)

The dichotomy that Citrine establishes between his inner and outer worlds here reveals itself as a vital opposition between childhood and adulthood. The contrast is clear, "maturity" and "realism," like "objects, actions and phenomena" are negative aspects of the world, "Childhood" with its transcendent Wordsworthian intimations of immortality is the great positive that Citrine has been fortunate enough to recapture.[3]

Citrine's affirmation of the value of childhood (an affirmation that corresponds to, and is as insubstantial as, Augie's "axial lines," or Herzog's "truth") accompanies a coming to terms with his own *childishness* that is unique in Bellow's canon. In Bellow's novels before *Humboldt's Gift,* the hero's childishness was presented in both a positive and negative aspect: positive, in that to be "naive," "innocent," childish and, by association, feminine was to be sensitive, truly understanding of the world, perceptive, and justifiably affirming; negative, in that a suspicion lingered around the hero that he was genuinely foolish, irresponsible, unable to see the world for what it really was, and hence doomed to remain out of control. In *Humboldt's Gift,* however, the struggle to grow up that so many Bellow heroes unwillingly go through has been abandoned. Financial dependency and familial lack of responsibility are unashamedly factors in Citrine's personality. Naturally "knowing" what he is like, Citrine can identify his type, but he has no desire to change: "How typical of me. The usual craving. I longed for someone to do the stations of the cross with me" (p. 70) Citrine remarks after one of his more tentative attempts to get some-one to help him out of a mess of his own contriving, but rather than being hard on himself for his own dependence, as Bellow's other heroes often are, Citrine is happy to occupy the status of a dependent. The role that Citrine plays in the "external," "adult" world does not overly bother him, for, in the world that matters to Citrine—the world of his own head—he is profoundly, so he believes, independent.

In *Mr. Sammler's Planet,* the hero's attempts to escape from the external world back into his own head are constantly thwarted by the interest that, against his better judgment, he continues to maintain in external phenomena and events. Moreover, the "world" in the shape of muggers, student radicals, and foolish daughters is prone to interfere with his private meditations. Charlie Citrine is even less interested in the world than Artur Sammler and his "evasions" are far more successful. Symbolically, Citrine's success in "escaping" the world is attested to by the identification that he sets up between himself and Harry Houdini.[4] Born, like Houdini, in Appleton, Wisconsin, Citrine, in his own way, conceives of himself as a "great Jewish escape artist" (p. 435).

Citrine's "success" can be gauged through a comparison of his and Sammler's reactions to the unwanted "impingements" of the world on their philosophical (or theosophical) progress. When Sammler is mugged, the event stimulates his consciousness, and brings the world back to him in full force; he "receive[s] from the crime the benefit of enlarged vision" (*Mr. Sammler's Planet,* p. 12), but when Citrine is humiliated by the criminal Cantabile—forced at gunpoint to watch Cantabile loosen his bowels—Citrine finds that

> In a situation like this I can always switch out and think about the human condition over all. (P. 83)

Citrine is an expert at what he calls "tun[ing] out" (p. 260). Whatever is happening to him in the external world seems almost irrelevant to what is going on inside him. Unlike Sammler, the world does not interfere too much with Citrine's private meditations. Rushed around by Cantabile, Citrine is able to concentrate his mind on Rudolf Steiner. The state that Citrine comes closer than any other Bellow hero to achieving is one that Bellow's Joseph outlines and lauds in the pages of his diary—a state in which one is free of the mind-polluting world (*Dangling Man,* p. 15).

However, if Citrine has managed to work up a greater indifference to the "external" world than any of Bellow's other heroes, he nevertheless "dangles" between the harmonic world within his own head and the discordant world outside. For, Citrine is transcendentally but not ascetically inclined. Moreover, the tendency of his personality is to bring trouble down in great bucketfuls over his head. Like all Bellow's Chicago types (with the exception of Joseph in *Dangling Man*), Citrine loves to hang out with tough guys and underworld figures. He plays poker with a small-time gangster—Rinaldo Cantabile—and ends up losing money, which he refuses to pay. Cantabile's first reaction is to smash up Citrine's Mercedes with a baseball bat—but this is only the beginning of his Cantabile problems. Concurrently, Citrine is involved with a glamorous young woman, Renata. With Renata, Citrine is holding out against marriage (another nonpayment of debts?) and eventually he pays for his prevarications. Renata ignominiously dumps him while they are holidaying in Spain and, to make matters worse, she leaves her son by a former marriage in Citrine's charge.

Nothing in Citrine's behavior seems to square with the kind of personality that one would imagine for a disciple of Dr. Rudolf Steiner. However, Citrine knows that he is drawn in contradictory directions and, like Herzog, he remains largely untroubled by the fact. Citrine also knows that he "asks for trouble. Why? . . . to turn me into deeper realms of peculiar but necessary thought" (p. 433). Aware that he is stimulated by crises, Citrine is further aware that his pervasive "dangling" has somehow caused him to be "not there." Unable to generate a sustaining interest in the world that he inhabits and unable to achieve the measure of transcendence that he claims to desire, Citrine recognizes that he is turning himself into an invisible man.

> I was aware that I used to think that I knew where I stood (taking the universe as a frame of reference). But I was mistaken. However, at least I could say that I had been spiritually efficient enough not to be crushed by ignorance. However, it was now apparent to me that I was neither of Chicago nor sufficiently beyond it, and that Chicago's material and daily interests and phenomena were neither actual and vivid enough or symbolically clear enough to me. So that I had

neither vivid actuality nor symbolic clarity and for the time
being I was utterly nowhere. (P. 260)

Most significantly, Citrine knows that he is detached from his
own behavior and from his own character and that such detachment is potentially mortifying.

Perhaps the fact that I had learned to stand apart from my
own frailties and the absurdities of my character might mean
that I was a little dead myself. (P. 439)

Charlie Citrine is his own best analyst. There is no reason
why Citrine should not be enormously self-conscious, but the
effect on Bellow's novel is harmful. In Bellow's early novels, the
energy of the hero's progress is derived from his ignorance of
the fact that he is prey to opposing desires that are mutually
exclusive. The constant struggle of all the heroes from Joseph
through Henderson is, ostensibly, to discover who they are.
Believing that they know what they want, order, harmony, and
so on, these heroes rend themselves over their inability to
achieve it. The effect on the later heroes of their profound
realization that they are irrevocably split personalities is to
transform them into the visiting consciousnesses that Bellow's
heroes have always threatened to become. Herzog, Sammler,
and, most emphatically, Citrine are happy to acknowledge and
accept the fact that they live in limbo. For Bellow, their content-
ment is clearly preferable to the anguish of his early heroes, but
at the same time the absence of a struggle effectively destroys
the dynamic of Bellow's fiction. Citrine, knowing who he is, has
lost the questing energy of Bellow's other heroes; consequently,
Citrine's experiences (like Herzog's and Sammler's) lose their
edge of meaning. In a sense, the inevitable pattern of a Bellow
novel that I have been trying to elucidate is well known to
Citrine. His vision and Bellow's visions have collided and
merged and having done so, much of the creative tension that
informs Bellow's novels seems to have been lost.

As if to compensate for the loss of thematic tension, the plot
of *Humboldt's Gift* is rather more complex than we have come to
expect in Bellow's more recent work. However, despite the in-
novatory and farcical twists and turns of the plot—which involve the ramifications of Citrine's discovering Humboldt's leg-
acy: two screenplays, one of which the two characters have

coauthored—the novel has an air of déjà vu about it. This familiarity stems mainly from the fact that *Humboldt's Gift* is largely peopled with characters whom we have met before under different names but in similar circumstances. *Humboldt's Gift* most vividly recalls *Herzog*, but it umbilically connected to all the other novels. Charlie Citrine, who in himself is very close to Moses Herzog, is divorced from the bitchy but beautiful Denise and embroiled in an affair with the sexy but demanding Renata.

Reincarnations of Madeleine and Ramona, Denise and Renata are not the only familiar figures. Citrine's brother Julius is Herzog's brother Shura only a few years on. Interestingly, even Rinaldo Cantabile, the charismatic hoodlum in *Humboldt's Gift*, shares qualities with "Rameau's nephew" (p. 174), a significant piece of characterization that links him to Bellow's earliest charlatan, Alf Steidler, who is also "un (personnage) composé de hauteur et de bassesse, de bonsens et de déraison" (*Dangling Man*, p. 127).

If Bellow's types are recognizable, and after all it must be concluded that all novelists have a stock cast of characters, the mode of their characterization is equally known. However, Bellow's tendency to define characters (both major and minor) by revealing or describing the contradictions inherent in their personalities has, in *Humboldt's Gift*, become a pervasive strategy.

Citrine himself is the most obvious case, and predictably it is the child/man foolish/wise aspects of his personality that seem to play the largest part in defining him. As with Herzog, Citrine devotes a great deal of time to pondering the problem of his character, and, again like Herzog, he is hard put to decide whether he is "a sensible person" or not (p. 64).[5] Citrine's ex-wife, Denise, is "a great beauty but not altogether human" (p. 40). Von Humboldt Fleisher, like King Dahfu, whom he resembles in many ways, is "below, shuffling comedy; above princeliness and dignity, a certain nutty charm" (11).[6]

Demmie Vonghel, one of Citrine's early loves, has a police record for "hubcap stealing, marijuana, sex offences . . ." (p. 19), but like Madeleine (*Herzog*), and Shula/Slawa (*Mr. Sammler's Planet*) she "believes in sin" (p. 29) and knows "three thousand bible verses" (p. 19). Even Renata, the "*Kama Sutra* dream-girl" (p. 191), who in her former life as Ramona is at least what she appears to be, in *Humboldt's Gift* turns out to be "by no means fully at ease in sex" (p. 191) and "sexually . . . not

all that she was cracked up to be" (p. 404). At one point in the
novel, Citrine describes his journalist friend Thaxter as "either
a kindly or a brutal man, and deciding which was a torment"
(p. 252). It is a torment that Bellow himself seems to undergo in
his characterizations.

Bellow defines characters, especially minor characters, in
what are really "black and white" sets of contradictions. As a
result Bellow's larger fictional world is bound to contradict his
hero's affirmative visions of that world. There can be no "life-
affirming," "kindly" men in Bellow's novels because, like Thaxter, such men are for the most part also potentially or actually
"brutal." Relentlessly, Bellow demonstrates how in his fictive
universe "nothing is but what is not." Citrine's agonizing over
Thaxter corresponds to Joseph's agonizing over the true nature of the world in *Dangling Man.* Joseph's "resolution" to his
"dangling" is to decide that the world is both good and malevo-
lent and therefore "it is neither" (*Dangling Man,* p. 29). Ultimately, in this way, the decision that Bellow's heroes reach is
that to dangle is to enact *the* human condition. That to dangle is
to be "utterly nowhere" (*Humboldt's Gift,* p. 260) is a torment
that can apparently only be relieved by transcending the world
or by detaching oneself from one's own personality. However,
in both Bellow's and Citrine's terms this seems to be a decision
to choose death over life. The choices that Bellow's heroes face
are difficult, at their most extreme they are impossible.

In terms of defining his own character, however, Citrine's
"choice" is not as difficult as it at first appears to be. For, like
Herzog's, Citrine's assessments of the "child" parts of him are
apparently harsh but, in terms of the novel's governing values,
positive. A "higher-thought clown" (p. 391), whose "emotional"
attachments are "childish" (p. 299), Citrine describes himself as
"in my own mind comically innocent" (p. 37); but Citrine, again
like Herzog, is almost proud of his characteristic foolishness.

> It mustn't be forgotten that I had been a complete idiot until
> I was forty and a partial idiot after that. I would always be
> something of an idiot. (P. 396)

The fact that Citrine's mainly grotesque contemporaries feel
that there is "a substantial suspicion of lunacy" (p. 406) hover-
ing around him, and that his hard-nosed, businessman brother

Julius thinks that he is "some sort of idiot" (p. 245) and "queerly undeveloped, [and] immature" (p. 354), only serves to shore up the reader's sense that Citrine's idiocy is really insight, his childishness profundity, his innocence wisdom, his femininity hard male intellectuality, his soft undevelopment strong emotion.

In *Humboldt's Gift*, the hero's insecurity over the child/ feminine aspects of his personality rarely manifests itself. Occasionally, however, incidents are related that seem designed to shore up Citrine's masculinity—for example, at one point in the novel Citrine recalls how while holidaying in New Mexico he saved a drowning man, Tigler, the macho, cowboy husband of Humboldt's widow. Tigler it transpires, cannot swim and the writer/city boy (i.e., girl) Citrine is transformed into a dominant male figure. But for the most part Citrine does not seem overly troubled by his affirmation of the child/woman part of him.

This becomes clear when we examine Citrine's relationship with Cantabile, which has homosexual overtones similar to that between Leventhal and Allbee in *The Victim*. Watching Cantabile loosen his bowels, Citrine feels that "he wanted to inflict a punishment on me but the result was only to make us more intimate" (p. 83). That something much more than hostility is passing between the two men becomes evident when Cantabile proposes that he, Citrine, and a woman engage in three-way sex. What is relevant, however, is the fact that in rejecting the idea, Citrine is not enraged by it.

> I was sophisticated enough to recognize that in what he proposed that we two should do with Polly there was a touch of homosexuality, but that wasn't very serious. (P. 287)

Leventhal is terrified by his own semiconscious attraction to Allbee, and by Allbee's attraction to him. Citrine, as with his "childishness," seems more at ease with his sexuality.

Citrine's relationship with Cantabile also helps to define the attraction of impotence and paralysis for the Bellow hero. A combination of Tamkin—he is "passionate about internal matters of very slight interest to any sensible person" (p. 64)—and one of Herzog's "Reality Instructors"—"All you people [i.e., intellectuals] are soft about realities" (p. 173)—Cantabile is also an aggressive, overpowering figure, and Citrine has known since first meeting him that "a natural connection" (p. 91) exists between them. This "natural connection" is vital to an understanding of Bellow's entire canon. Because he "dangles" Citrine is as the mercy of dominating "father figures."

> The reason why the Ulicks [Julius] of this world (and also the Cantabiles) had such sway over me was that they knew their desires clearly. (P. 396)

The connection between Citrine's brother and Cantabile emphasizes the fundamental sameness of the male relationships that Citrine sets up for himself. "Dangling," Citrine is drawn, like almost all Bellow's heroes, to conative, determined individuals who tend to make him feel impotent and paralyzed, and in whose company he can only behave like a child. But, remarkably, Citrine (like all the heroes) manages to transform this impotence into something positive—it is one of his, and Bellow's heroes', most important and vitally self-preserving achievements. When Cantabile forces Citrine to accompany him to the top of a half-built skyscraper, tread the open floors, and look down from a dizzying height—a scene that explicitly symbolizes Citrine's "Bellovian" impotence—Citrine's reaction is surprisingly positive.

> But however scared and harassed, my sensation loving soul was also gratified. I knew that it took too much to gratify me. The gratification-threshold of my soul had risen too high. I must bring it down again. It was excessive. I must, I knew, change everything. (P. 102)

At the risk of "going too far," I would like to suggest that the "sensation" that Citrine loves is not so much the danger, but the complete humiliation and paralysis. Like Artur Sammler and the black pickpocket, Herzog and Madeleine, Henderson and Dahfu with the lion, Wilhelm and his father, Augie and Simon, Leventhal and Allbee, and Joseph and the Army, Citrine derives his energy, his "gratification," from his relationship with a figure to whom he is deeply attracted and who can offer him only impotence. For Bellow's heroes, paradoxically, a productive crisis is one that is paralyzing.[7]

The condition that Bellow's heroes aspire toward is thus, figuratively, that of a child. Carried along, like passengers on a train, by the energy and power of driven domineering brothers, wives, friends, parents, or acquaintances, Bellow's heroes can convince themselves that they are no longer responsible for their own actions. Divorce problems, money problems, family problems, in fact the "adult" world altogether, is in abeyance while the hero is in the hands of a Simon, Dahfu, or Cantabile. In Bellow's world, this "childhood" state is Edenic not because it is free but because it is controlled and to a certain extent, imprisoning.

Charlie Citrine has what he calls a "child's soul" (p. 3), but, problematically for him, he is for the most part surrounded by characters who insist on being taken in by, and hence responding to, his adult body. As a result, like all Bellow's heroes, he searches out authoritarian, dominating father figures—who he knows will treat him like a child. Most of Bellow's heroes, having done this, at some stage rebel and attempt to reassert their "adult" independence, but Citrine is not interested in achieving "external" independence. The world that he sets up to inhabit is in form if not in content (Citrine has deep and sophisticated thoughts) a complete paradigm of a child's world. Internally independent in his own world, Citrine is happy to remain dependent and "controlled" in the external world. Citrine can revel in his dependence because his inner freedom is autonomous and secure: a child's private inner world that is a sustaining haven.

In a revealing conversation with Von Humboldt Fleisher, who is himself one of Citrine's mentors and father figures, Fleisher perceptively notes

> I think you may be one of those Axel types that only cares about inner inspiration, no connection with the actual world. The actual world can kiss your ass, . . . You leave it to poor bastards like me to think about matters like money and status and success and failure and social problems and politics. You don't give a damn for such things. (P. 122)

"If true," Citrine replies, "why is that so bad?" (p. 122). Citrine's feeling is that "to be fully conscious of oneself as an individual is also to be separated from all else" (p. 203), but it more accurately seems to be the case that Citrine's "power to remain unaffected by anything whatsoever" (p. 203) is only activated when, like Augie, he has "given himself up to another guy's schemes." Humboldt, sounding in the above quotation almost like Dr. Adler, Tommy Wilhelm's father, has somehow

taken on Citrine's "adult" responsibilities; and however unconsciously, Citrine, like all Bellow's heroes, has sought him out
because that is precisely what he wants.

Interestingly Citrine's own interpretation of his attraction to
Humboldt, Cantabile, and characters like them seems almost a
formulaic outline of Bellow's method of relating minor to major characters.

> By and by it became apparent that he had acted as my agent.
> I myself, a nicely composed person, had had Humboldt
> wildly expressing himself on my behalf, satisfying some of
> my longings. This explained my liking for certain individu-
> als—Humboldt, or George Swiebel, or even someone like
> Cantabile. (P. 107)

However, Citrine's insight does not go so far as to see that
Humboldt, Swiebel, and Cantabile, acting out the "wild" and
absurd aspects of Citrine's personality are also surrogate
fathers, much in the manner of Einhorn, Sandor Himmelstein,
or Tamkin. Along with "acting out" Citrine's "chaotic" qualities,
they respond to his deeply problematic and ambivalent desire
to become an adult.

When Citrine is required to take responsibility for his own
actions, as in his endless legal conflict with Denise, when he is in
a situation where he must defend and watch out for himself,
things begin to get problematic.

In chambers with the vindictive Judge Urbanovich, Citrine
tries to remove himself mentally from the proceedings

> Anthroposophy was having definite effects. I couldn't take
> any of this too hard. Otherworldiness tinged it all and every
> little while my spirit seemed to disassociate itself. It left me
> and passed out the window. . . . (P. 231)

But when the cynical "reality instructor" judge reminds Citrine
of his "responsibilities," the spell is broken.

> "Mr. Citrine, . . . you've led a more or less bohemian life.
> Now you've had a taste of marriage, the family, middle-class
> institutions, and you want to drop out. But we can't allow you
> to dabble like that."
> Suddenly my detachment ended and I found myself in a
> state. (Pp. 231–32)

When Citrine is confronted by the results of his "adult" behavior, what is brought home to him is the fact that no matter how hard he tries he cannot escape the fate of a "dangling man." In *Humboldt's Gift*, Citrine dangles between an inner world where all is spiritual order and an external world where "chaos" is a function of any kind of adult responsibility or behavior.

Citrine, who is, as he puts it, "just a beginner in the theosophical kindergarten" (p. 356) has, as Renata puts it, "spen[t] years trying to dope [his] way out of the human condition" (p. 430). "When," Citrine wonders, "would I at last rise above this stuff, the accidental, the merely phenomenal, the wastefully and randomly human, and be fit to enter higher worlds?" (p. 291). Not so long, one might reply, as Citrine remains a prisoner of what he calls "personal and erotic bondage" (p. 356). Needing the pleasures of sex and the gratification of his personal instincts, Citrine is hard put to accede to the "adult" demands that civilized society makes upon him in his roles as husband, parent, or just plain lover. Like Augie March, for Charlie Citrine "the main bonds of attachment are death ropes" (*The Adventures of Augie March*, p. 322).

Forced, when he is without a protective father figure, to take responsibility for his own actions, Citrine detaches himself from his own behavior either by "elevating such mean considerations to the theoretical level" (p. 181) or by theosophically observing his own "circumscribed self from without" (p. 393). Intellectual abstraction and theosophical transcendentalism are both, however, as we have seen, connotatively deathly for Citrine. Dangling between "Detachment" or "Transcendence" and the pressing demands of daily life, Citrine chooses neither. Metaphorically, it seems Citrine is dangling between Death (which after all seems only an attenuation of transcendence) and Life.

Interestingly, in this respect, one of the thematic strains that runs through *Humboldt's Gift* is derived from the hero's meditations on the relationship between sleep and waking. Like Eugene Henderson, Citrine wants to awaken his slumbering spirit.[8] But, for Citrine, "wakefulness" will not return him happily to a world of social community, but will rather enable him to break through into a transcendent inner world. For Citrine, daily life is sleep and, paradoxically, he does not want to wake up into the bad dream of the adult world but into the spiritual light of a nonmaterial universe.

The "rending" of Bellow's heroes seems, with Charlie Citrine, to have reached its terminal stage. Reflection on the relation between Citrine's inner and outer worlds leads to reflection on the relation of death to life; that death projectively appears to be the ultimate "order" for Citrine and life to be unremitting "chaos" is an additional factor in explaining why he finds it so difficult to choose between them.

Increasingly the heroes of Bellow's late novels have championed the spiritual world over the material world. The diminishing importance of earthly phenomena for these heroes has, to a certain extent, lessened the pain of their inner dichotomies. However, less rent than Bellow's early heroes, Herzog, Sammler, and Citrine yet remain characters who are torn between the worlds of transcendent peace to which they aspire and the harsh unaccomodating worlds of the quotidian that they inhabit. Unable to take what they want—whether that desire is to achieve external order, internal order, or transcendence of the world—and drawn to chaotic marriages, spurious and dangerous adventures, and relationships with criminals and bitches, Herzog, Sammler, and Citrine remain recognizable "dangling men" who are, because of their detachment from their own behavior, less painfully tortured than their predecessors.

Flanked by characters who both extend their own inner conflicts (Gruner and the pickpocket, Cantabile and Durnwald) and are themselves defined by contradictions (Madeleine, Gruner, Denise, Thaxter et al.), Bellow's later heroes inhabit a world that is self-reflexive, centripetal, and apparently designed to shore up their own visions of the world as irretrievably split.

In his first five novels, Bellow concluded with images of men who were essentially alone but searching for community. Joseph in his room is about to enter the army. Leventhal at the theater with his wife is beginning life anew, Augie driving north in Europe is hoping to find whatever it is that he seeks, Henderson circling the plane is making ready for his new life. In *Herzog, Mr. Sammler's Planet,* and *Humboldt's Gift* we find quite a different situation. Herzog, alone in his Berkshire garden has "nothing. Not a single word" (*Herzog,* p. 341) for anyone. Sammler, in a hospital morgue is praying to himself. We last see Citrine at a cemetery where he is witnessing the reburial in a proper grave of the pauper-poet Humboldt. At the graveside, Citrine notices a single spring crocus, a symbolic antidote to the gloom of death. These three characters, Herzog, Sammler, and Citrine, searching for nothing, content with the little flowers of meaning that they discover in the debris of their lives, celebrate only what they have: unique minds and a solipsism that Bellow's other heroes claim to want to rid themselves of.

Increasingly aware of everything about themselves and the worlds that they inhabit, Herzog, Sammler, and Citrine seem to articulate Bellow's own vision as well as enacting a part in it. Moreover, they are increasingly autobiographical figures, harder and harder to detach from the artist who is putting words into their mouths. The effect on the novels of this narrowing of paths is to render them somehow "closed." *Humboldt's Gift,* in particular, has a terminal air about it. For there is little fictional "tension" in the novel. Charlie Citrine, who "knows" the static contraries of both his own personality and of the world that he inhabits, fails to be energized by them. Citrine has no quest, and, consequently, *Humboldt's Gift* has no real dialectical thrust. This is partly because Citrine's self-knowledge coalesces with the informing vision of the novel in which he appears, and it is partly because he is not so much an imagined character—with the distance and tension that implies—as an avatar of his creator.[9]

In *Humboldt's Gift,* Bellow seems finally to have consumed himself. It is perhaps for this reason that when he came to write *The Dean's December,* Bellow made an effort to eschew autobiography, at least on the surface, in the creation of his central character. Albert Corde, with his classy Huguenot Irish-American background, turns out to have the mind of a Herzog or Citrine—an enclosed complex mind that is its own place, provides its own energy supply, and spins alone in the increasingly opaque and threatening world.

Notes

Introduction

1. Isaiah Berlin, *The Hedgehog and The Fox* (1953; reprint, New York: Simon & Schuster, 1966), pp. 1–2.

2. In an essay on *The Adventures of Augie March* and *Herzog,* Robert Shulman asserts that "Bellow . . . revealingly belongs to a line of descent (and dissent) characterized by the intellectual comedy and expansive prose of writers like Rabelais, Burton, Sterne and Joyce." "The Style of Bellow's Comedy," *PMLA* 83 (March 1968): 110. Tony Tanner compares Bellow to Whitman and Dreiser, finding that he shares with these writers a "voracious appetite for the teeming stuff around [him]. The habit of simply naming long lists of things should not be dismissed as mere cataloguing but seen for what it is—an awed accumulation . . . a delighted revelling in the profuse evidence of an incredibly fecund creation." *Saul Bellow* (Edinburgh: Oliver & Boyd, 1965), p. 13.

3. Saul Bellow, interview with Gordon Lloyd Harper, in *Writers at Work: The Paris Review Interviews,* Third Series (New York: Viking, 1967), p. 196.

4. Tony Tanner's short book *Saul Bellow,*the first full-length work ever to be published on Bellow, set a pattern of critical response that has rarely been deviated from in the last eighteen years. Summing up Bellow's vision of the world, Tanner remarks "He [Bellow] neither capitulates to the contemporary world nor does he renounce it. The adventure all takes place between those two rigid, extreme reactions. Aware of all that is corrupt and destructive in the modern world, Bellow refused to traffic in pessimism. What he said of Joyce Cary's writing applies to his own: '[I]t accepts the contemporary, it defends the possibilities of man in the present, denies that it is so very bad to be what we are or that we are born to be condemned with the times.'" Tanner, *Saul Bellow,* p. 15. John J. Clayton, whose book on Bellow seems to have become something of a touchstone for Bellow's American critics, entitles his opening chapter "In Desperate Affirmation." For Clayton, Bellow "rejects the denigration of the ordinary life of the individual and tries to show in his fiction the possibilities for finding meaning in such lives. In all his novels the defense of human dignity and human possibilities, even in a dehumanized age, stands central." John J. Clayton, *Saul Bellow: In Defense of Man* (Bloomington: Indiana University Press, 1968), p. 24. A key word in Bellow criticism, *affirmation* crops up time and again. For Ihab Hassan, Bellow's novels are an "affirmation of reality." Ihab Hassan, *Radical Innocence: Studies in the Contemporary American Novel* (1961; reprint, New York: Harper & Row, 1966), p. 290. While M. G. Porter has found that Bellow's novels may be characterized by their "affirmative tone of celebration," the title of Porter's book accurately

suggests his assessment of Bellow's vision. M. Gilbert Porter, *Whence the Power? The Artistry and Humanity of Saul Bellow* (Columbia: University of Missouri Press, 1974), p. 196. More recently Malcolm Bradbury has placed Bellow's novels "in the same affirmative tradition: as the late work of Faulkner, Hemingway, Steinbeck and Sinclair Lewis." *Saul Bellow* (London and New York: Methuen, 1982), p. 22.

5. For Howard Harper, "[E]ach of [Bellow's] novels is a brilliant and original conception; each creates its own unique view of the human condition, in which the form itself becomes meaning." *Desperate Faith: A Study of Bellow, Salinger, Mailer, Baldwin and Updike* (Chapel Hill: North Carolina Press, 1967), pp. 62–63.

6. Bellow's heroes "move towards something . . . euphoric and affirmative," writes Tony Tanner. *Saul Bellow*, p. 7. Similarly Marcus Klein asserts, "Bellow's characters . . . remain much the same . . . [a]nd they face problems which are reducible to a single problem: to meet with a strong sense of self the sacrifices of self demanded by social circumstance. Alienation, the sense of separate and unconciliating identity, must travel to accommodation." *After Alienation* (New York: World Publishing, 1970), p. 34. Throughout his chapter on Bellow, *accommodation* for Klein is almost synonymous with Tanner's *affirmation*. Most recently, Eusebio Rodrigues has tried to demonstrate how the Bellow protagonist is "always in search of the human" and how "the novels clearly suggest that they are projections of Bellow's own arduous climb towards true humanness." Eusebio L. Rodrigues, *Quest for the Human: An Exploration of Saul Bellow's Fiction* (East Brunswick, N.J., London and Toronto: Associated University Presses, 1981), p. 10.

7. Most critics have used Bellow's speeches, interviews, and discursive prose to shore up their interpretations of the novels as "life-affirming." See, for example, Tanner, *Saul Bellow*, pp. 2–15; Clayton, *Saul Bellow*, pp. 3–29 *passim;* Harper, *Desperate Faith*, p. 63; Keith Opdahl, *The Novels of Saul Bellow: An Introduction* (University Park: Pennsylvania State University Press, 1967), p. 24.

8. See Bellow, *Writers at Work*, p. 196; "The Nobel Lecture," *The American Scholar* 46 (Summer 1977): 325; and Saul Bellow, "Some Notes on Recent American Fiction," in *The Novel Today*, ed. Malcolm Bradbury (1963; reprint, Manchester and London: Manchester University Press and Fontana), p. 66.

9. Bellow, "Some Notes on Recent American Fiction," p. 62.

10. Bellow, *Writers at Work*, pp. 195 and 196.

11. Lionel Trilling, *Sincerity and Authenticity* (London: Oxford University Press, 1972), pp. 39 and 41.

12. Gabriel Josipovici, *The Lessons of Modernism and Other Essays* (London: Macmillan, 1977), p. 64.

13. Tony Tanner, *Saul Bellow*, p. 106. Irving Howe, *The Critical Point* (New York: Delta, 1973), p. 123.

14. The exception that proves the rule is Minna Corde, wife of Albert Corde, the hero of *The Dean's December*. She is Bellow's only constant, loyal, loving, and *lovable* wife and for once the hero is not led to seek out a mistress. In note 2 to my chapter on *The Dean's December*, I suggest a reason for this unusual state of Bellovian affairs.

15. Malcolm Bradbury, "Saul Bellow's *Herzog*," *Critical Quarterly* 7 (Autumn 1965): 271.

16. Ibid., p. 274 and p. 278.

17. Tony Tanner, *City of Words: American Fiction 1950–1970* (London: Jonathan Cape, 1971), p. 17.

Chapter 1. *The Dean's December*

1. Tony Tanner has used the term *fictionalized recall* to describe the "genre" of which *Herzog* is representative. He includes *Portnoy's Complaint* among those novels in which "the adoption of a different name for the re-membering self gives the author the license to make such distortions and suppressions . . . as seem to him desirable . . . for the particular vision and diagnosis he wishes to articulate." In *City of Words*, p. 295.

2. It is interesting that the only two of Bellow's heroes to achieve anything like a happy marriage are his two gentile protagonists, Eugene Henderson and Albert Corde. In all Bellow's novels "Jewishness" seems to carry the metaphoric weight of "limitation" and marriage is always conceived of as imprisoning. In *The Dean's December*, Bellow seems to help himself to imagine a successful marriage by allowing the hero involved to forgo the extra burden of Jewishness. In terms of his own life, as many reviewers have been happy to note, Bellow, if *The Dean's December* is anything to go by, has finally achieved a happy marriage of his own.

3. Mark Schechner, "The Dean's Despair," Boston Phoenix, 2 February 1982, p. 2.

4. Norman Mailer, *Cannibals and Christians* (1964; reprint, New York: Delta, 1966), p. 127.

5. John W. Aldridge has argued that "Bellow's handling of these people [minor characters in Bellow's canon] constantly verges on caricature. In fact there are moments when they seem to exist solely as verbal abstractions, creations of merely adjectival intensity." "The Complacency of *Herzog*," in *Saul Bellow and the Critics*, ed. Irving Malin (New York: New York University Press, 1967), p. 208.

Chapter 2. *Dangling Man*

1. By naming the character "Gesell" Bellow may well be playing on the German word *Gesellschaft* meaning "society."

2. Bradbury, *Saul Bellow*, p. 36.

3. Leslie Fiedler found *Dangling Man* to be "unlike any American war book before or since," attributing its uniqueness to Bellow's realization that "for his generation the war was an anticlimax . . . too foreknown from a score of older novels to be really lived." *Collected Essays* vol. 2 (New York: Stein & Day, 1971), pp. 59–60. For Malcolm Bradbury *Dangling Man* "captures not only the wartime atmosphere but the haunting crisis about political bad faith that developed during the years of cold war, rising materialism and what Daniel Bell has called 'the end of ideology.' " *Saul Bellow*, p. 36.

4. Maxwell Geismar, *American Moderns: From Rebellion to Conformity* 1958; reprint, New York: Hill & Wang, 1964), p. 212.

5. Ihab Hassan, *Radical Innocence*, p. 212.

6. Irving Malin, *Jews and Americans*Carbondale and Edwardsville: Southern Illinois University Press, 1965), p. 23.

Chapter 3. *The Victim*

1. Keith Opdahl, *The Novels of Saul Bellow*, p. 174.
2. John Gardner, *On Moral Fiction* (New York: Basic Books, 1978), p. 91.
3. Ibid., p. 92.
4. See Jay Nash and Ron Offen, "Saul Bellow," *Literary Times,* December 1964, p. 10. In both novels, the "double" attempts to murder the hero after he has slept in the hero's apartment, and both sets of relationships have what Opdahl calls an "overtone of oppressive, homosexual affection" (Opdahl, p. 173). Full discussions of the parallels between *The Eternal Husband* and *The Victim* can be found in the critical work of Marcus Klein, John Jay Clayton, and Keith Opdahl (see bibliography).
5. Norman Podhoretz, *Doings and Undoings: The Fifties and After in American Writing* (New York: Farrar, Straus & Giroux, 1964), p. 214.
6. John Jay Clayton, *Saul Bellow: In Defense of Man*, p. 151.
7. Tony Tanner, *Saul Bellow*, p. 36.
8. Diana Trilling, review in *Nation* 166 (3 January 1948):24; Maxwell Geismar, *American Moderns*, p. 216; Leslie Fiedler, *Collected Essays* 2 : 60; Says Bradbury, "*The Victim* is a book about the oblique, angular bonds of moral responsiblity. . . ." (*Saul Bellow*, p. 44), while for John Jay Clayton "the theme of [the] book is the casting off of self-imposed burdens by [the hero's] learning to accept himself." *Saul Bellow: In Defense of Man*, p. 139.
9. Bellow, *Writers at Work*, p. 182.
10. Opdahl, *The Novels of Saul Bellow*, p. 52.
11. According to Bellow, *Dangling Man* and *The Victim* did not give him a form in which he felt comfortable. "A writer," he says, "should be able to express himself easily, naturally, copiously in a form which frees his mind, his energies. Why should he hobble himself with formalities? With a borrowed sensibility, with the desire to be 'correct.'" *Writers at Work*, p. 183.

Introduction to Part Two

1. Robert Boyers has asserted that "[t]here is in Bellow's entire fictional output no convincing illumination of the nature of normal sexual relations in American society. . . . [T]he female character who has most to do with the direction taken by the novel's protagonist is in the tradition of the American bitch goddess, a figure whom we need never consider too closely, for we know she is a mere creature of those dire fantasies which we maintain to justify our inexplicable terrors." *Excursions: Selected Literary Essays* (New York: Kennikat Press, 1977), p. 116. See also Vivian Gornick, "Why do these Men Hate Women? American Writers and Misogyny," *Village Voice,* 6 December 1976, pp. 12–15. The "Men" in question are Saul Bellow, Norman Mailer, Henry Miller, and Philip Roth. Interestingly, Victoria Sullivan has defended Bellow against the charge of sexism and attempted to make a case for the richness and depth of his portrayal of women characters. See Victoria Sullivan, "The

Battle of the Sexes in Three Bellow Novels," in *Saul Bellow: A Collection of Critical Essays,* ed. Earl Rovit (Englewood Cliffs, N.J.: Prentice-Hall, 1975), pp. 101–14.

Chapter 4. *The Adventures of Augie March*

1. Harvey Breit, "Talk with Saul Bellow," *New York Times Book Review,* 20 September 1953, p. 22.

2. Saul Bellow, *Writers at Work: The Paris Review Interviews* 3d Series, p. 182.

3. Allen Guttman, *The Jewish Writer in America: Assimilation and the Crisis of Identity* (New York: Oxford University Press, 1971), p. 190; Robert Shulman, "The Style of Bellow's Comedy," p. 109; Richard Chase, "The Adventures of Saul Bellow: The Progress of a Novelist," in *Saul Bellow and the Critics,* ed. Irving Malin (New York: New York University Press, 1967), p. 28; Eusebio Rodrigues, *Quest for the Human,* p. 75; Malcolm Bradbury, *Saul Bellow,* p. 50.

4. Twelve years after he wrote *The Adventures of Augie March,* Bellow himself had second thoughts about the style he had developed in the novel. "I took off many . . . restraints. I think I took off too many and went too far, but I was feeling the excitement of discovery. I had just increased my freedom and like any emancipated plebian I abused it at once." *Writers at Work,* p. 182.

5. Shulman, "The Style of Bellow's Comedy," p. 110.

6. John Berryman, *The Freedom of the Poet* (New York: Farrar, Straus & Giroux, 1976), p. 223.

7. Robert Penn Warren, "The Man With No Commitments," *New Republic,* 2 November 1953; Tony Tanner, *Saul Bellow,* p. 55.

8. For Norman Podhoretz, Bellow, when writing *The Adventures of Augie March,* "looked back to . . . the picaresque. . . . And the fact that one of the greatest of all American novels (whose title is echoed by his own) itself derived from this tradition made it all the more obvious that he had hit upon the right mode for a novel that was setting out to discover America and the American dream anew." *Doings and Undoings,* pp. 216–17. For Leslie Fiedler, the character Augie March is "Huckleberry Finn reimagined by Saul Bellow for the survivors of the thirties." *Waiting for the End* (1964: reprint, New York: Penguin, 1967), p. 95.

9. Bellow, *Writers at Work,* p. 191.

10. Tanner, *Saul Bellow,* p. 46.

11. Albert J. Guerard, "Saul Bellow and the Activists: *The Adventures of Augie March,*" *Southern Review* 3 (July 1967): 583.

Chapter 5. *Seize the Day*

1. Some critics have tended to play down Wilhelm's pathetic character and have concentrated instead on his vulnerability in the face of a hostile father and hostile world. Tony Tanner, for example writes that like Augie March "Wilhelm . . . lives in a world of Machiavellians, but this time they exert a real and sinister power. . . . Tommy Wilhelm meets the world's opposition full-face." *Saul Bellow,* pp. 58–59. For Keith Opdahl, "Wilhelm is . . . the victim of his societies' peculiar emotional sterility." *The Novels of Saul Bellow,* p. 108.

In these versions Wilhelm is more sinned against than sinning. Such emphases open the door to an interpretation of the novella as "life-affirming"— Wilhelm joining the long line of Bellow heroes to affirm the values of life in a world that refuses to listen.

2. Daniel Weiss, "Caliban on Prospero: A Psychoanalytic Study on the Novel *Seize The Day*, by Saul Bellow," in *Saul Bellow and the Critics*, ed. Irving Malin, p. 121. I would further suggest that Wilhelm's attachment to Venice is not only because he is a father but also because he identifies with him as a child. "He [Venice] was the obscure failure of an aggressive and powerful clan. As such he had the greatest sympathy from Wilhelm" (p. 20).

3. Bellow's central text throughout the novel appears to be Montaigne's essay "On the Affection of Fathers for their Children." "Many a parent is very liberal in supplying his children with toys but becomes close-fisted over the slightest sum that they need once they are of age. It really looks as if our jealousy at seeing them come out and enjoy the world when we are on the point of leaving it, makes us more sparing and niggardly towards them. We are vexed that they should tread on our heels, as if to urge our departures. But if this were something to be feared, the order of things decreeing that they cannot, in fact, be nor live except at the expense of our being and our life, we should never have allowed ourselves to be fathers." Montaigne, *Essays*, trans. J. M. Cohen (1958; reprint, Penguin 1978) p. 140.

4. Allen Guttmann, *The Jewish Writer in America*, p. 200. See, for example, Howard Harper. "In the context of the absurd, the ultimate and only universal reality is death. In the face of this anonymous corpse, Wilhelm has seen himself and humanity. The truth 'deeper than sorrow' is the recognition of this ultimate reality, man's inevitable fate. In that fate Wilhelm discovers his own humanity. And the 'heart's ultimate need' is the acceptance of that truth and a commitment to life in spite of, indeed in defiance of, the lack of any ultimate meaning." *Desperate Faith*, p. 37. See also M. Gilbert Porter, *Whence The Power? The Artistry and Humanity of Saul Bellow*, pp. 124–25. Porter virtually repeats Harper's argument.

5. Opdahl, *The Novels of Saul Bellow*, p. 67.

6. Tanner, *Saul Bellow*, p. 67.

7. Marcus Klein has argued that *Seize The Day* charts "[t]he progress of Bellow's sensible hero from alienation to accommodation . . . from isolation to affirmation of ordinary life in the world." *After Alienation*, p. 41. For John Jay Clayton, "*Seize The Day* is . . . an affirmation of human life; an affirmation of the possibility that the 'salesman' need not go to his 'death,' need not live a life given to him by others and follow a masochistic strategy to preserve his childish self." *Saul Bellow: In Defense of Man*, p. 28.

8. Weiss, "Caliban on Prospero," p. 128.

Chapter 6. *Henderson the Rain King*

1. Mary Douglas, *Purity and Danger* (London: Routledge & Kegan Paul, 1966), p. 2.

2. Ibid.

3. Ibid., pp. 4–6.

4. Marcus Klein, *After Alienation*, p. 54.

5. Howard M. Harper, *Desperate Faith,* p. 41.
6. Eusebio Rodrigues, *Quest for the Human,* p. 115.
7. Norman Podhoretz, *Doings and Undoings,* p. 225.
8. John Jay Clayton has noted the hint of "daffy" in Dahfu's name. *Saul Bellow: In Defense of Man,* p. 168.
9. Norman Mailer, *Cannibals and Christians,* p. 127.
10. David Galloway, "Culture Making: The Recent Works of Saul Bellow," in *Saul Bellow and His Work,* ed. Edmond Schraepen (Brussels: Free University of Brussels Press, 1978), p. 56.
11. Norman Podhoretz wrote at the time of the book's publication, "The note of affirmation on which Mr. Bellow closes is not in the least convincing, and altogether lacks the force to counteract the magnificent passages of anguish and despair that fill the body of the book." Review of *Henderson the Rain King* in the *New York Herald Tribune Book Review,* 22 February 1959, p. 3. Tony Tanner has noted that "[o]ne forgets the unresolved issues of the book in the invigorating beauty of the last scene." *Saul Bellow,* p. 80.

Chapter 7. *Herzog*

1. Richard Poirier has complained at length about Bellow's self-protective first person narrative. "Allowing no version of the alleged betrayals other than Herzog's, Bellow still must protect his hero's claims to guiltlessness by a process all the more ultimately effective for being paradoxical: he lets Herzog's suffering issue forth less as accusations against others than as self-contempt for his having been cozened by them. . . . Bellow can thus operate snugly (and smugly) within the enclosure of his hero's recollections, assured . . . that he has anticipated and therefore forestalled antagonistic intrusions from outside." "*Herzog* or Bellow in Trouble," in *Saul Bellow: A Collection of Critical Essays,* ed. Earl Rovit, p. 85.
2. Saul Bellow, *Writers at Work,* pp. 193–94.
3. Irving Howe has argued that "there is no pretense in this novel that we are being shown a world which exists, self-sufficient, apart from the neurotic inflammations of the central character." *The Critical Point,* p. 123. But, again unlike the hero of *Portnoy's Complaint,* Herzog does not come across as a character whose neuroses have caused him to distort reality. When Herzog images Madeleine as both whore and beauty, slut and courtesan, we tend to accept his characterizations as accurate. If we were to view Herzog's assessments as no different from Portnoy's ravings, the novel would become a very different type of comedy.
4. Jane Howard, "Mr. Bellow Considers His Planet," *Life,* 3 April 1970, pp. 57–60.

Chapter 8. *Mr. Sammler's Planet*

1. Malcolm Bradbury, *Saul Bellow,* p. 81.
2. The first three quotations are from John Jay Clayton, *Saul Bellow: In Defense of Man,* pp. 254, 253, and 260, respectively.
3. Max F. Schulz "Mr. Bellow's Perigree, or, The Lowered Horizons of *Mr.*

Sammlers Planet," in *Contemporary American-Jewish Literature: Critical Essays,* ed. Irving Malin (Bloomington: Indiana University Press, 1973), p. 132.

4. For some of Bellow's comments on the sixties, see for example Bellow's essay "Culture Now: Some Animadversions, Some Laughs," where he not only attacks the New Left but all those "brutal profs and bad tempered ivy-league sodomites" who romanticize the "bohemianizing" of American society: *Modern Occasions* 1 (Winter 1971): 162–78. For Bellow's comments on late-sixties feminism, his interview with Jane Howard is representative. "Women," says Bellow, "show all the characteristics of slaves in revolt. . . . They are prone to the excesses of the newly freed." "Mr. Bellow Considers His Planet," *Life,* 3 April 1970, p. 60. Ben Siegel's comment is from "Saul Bellow and Mr. Sammler: Absurd Seekers of High Qualities," in *Saul Bellow: A Collection of Critical Essays,* ed. Earl Rovit (Englewood Cliffs, New Jersey: Prentice-Hall, 1975), p. 126.

5. Brigitte Scheer-Schazler has described *Mr. Sammler's Planet* as "indicative of Bellow's present inclination for the 'non-fiction philosophical novel.'" *Saul Bellow* (New York: Frederich Ungar, 1972), p. 128.

Chapter 9. *Humboldt's Gift*

1. Bellow's friend, the poet Delmore Schwartz, is, as James Atlas's biography *Delmore Schwartz* documents, the model for Von Humboldt Fleisher. The composite Fleisher, I would suggest, may also contain some of the characteristics of Bellow's close friend John Berryman. *Delmore Schwartz: The Life of an American Poet* (New York: Farrar, Straus & Giroux, 1977), p. ix.

2. John Berryman's "Dream Song 150" reports the guilt-provoking incident repeated by Citrine in *Humboldt's Gift.* The poem is the fifth in a series of twelve elegies that Berryman wrote for Schwartz. See John Berryman, *The Dream Songs* (New York: Farrar, Straus & Giroux, 1969), p. 169.

3. It may be pushing things too far but it seems to me that Citrine's descriptions of the year he spent as a child in a TB ward (a time also recorded in *Herzog* and no doubt an actual experience of Bellow's) are profoundly revealing in this respect.

> I think that my disease of the lungs passed over into an emotional disorder so that I sometimes felt, and still feel, poisoned by eagerness, a congestion of tender impulses together with fever and enthusiastic dizziness. Owing to the T.B. I connected breathing with joy, and owing to the gloom of the ward I connected joy with light, and owing to my irrationality I related light on the walls to light inside me. (P. 65)

Citrine's memories seem to explain not only the familiar "passionate dizziness" of Bellow's adult heroes (for example, *Herzog,* p. 231) and the obscure insights that Bellow's other heroes derive from seeing light on walls (*Henderson the Rain King,* p. 101; *Mr. Sammler's Planet,* p. 298) but also the "childish," "naive" affirmations of all Bellow's heroes. For the young Citrine (Bellow?) simply, *breathing is joy.* Interestingly this initial free and simple affirmation is reached while the hero is "paralyzed" in a hospital bed.

4. Herzog too is fascinated by Houdini (*Herzog,* p. 177).

5. Much of Citrine's reminiscing and musing is done while he is lying on a

couch in his Chicago apartment. The parallel with Herzog is emphasized when Citrine's meditations are interrupted by the arrival of Renata, who calls through on the intercom. In *Herzog* it is Ramona's phone call that wakes Herzog from his reverie (*Herzog,* p. 150).

6. Charismatic, impressive and articulate, Humboldt holds precisely the same attraction for Citrine as Dahfu for Henderson, but, as in the latter case, Citrine is more interested in Humboldt's magnetic personality than in what he actually has to say. "If you could believe Humboldt (and I couldn't). . . ." (p. 27).

7. Again, Citrine's TB experience seems formative and defining.

8. References to Rip Van Winkle abound in *Humboldt's Gift*. When Citrine takes his two children to a Christmas pageant, *Rip Van Winkle* is given as a curtain raiser. The play provokes Citrine to wonder "What would I have *done* if I hadn't been asleep in spirit for so long?" (p. 292).

9. Frank D. McConnell has noted how in *Humboldt's Gift* "the episodes alternate between . . . autobiography and elegy." *Four Postwar American Novelists: Bellow, Mailer, Barth and Pynchon* (Chicago: University of Chicago Press, 1977), p. 49. As Tony Tanner has written, "It is no secret that much of Herzog's experience is Bellow's. . . ." *City of Words,* p. 295.

Select Bibliography

1. Works by Saul Bellow

The Adventures of Augie March. New York: Viking, 1953.

"Culture Now." *Modern Occasions* 1 (Winter 1971): 162–78.

Dangling Man. New York: Vanguard, 1944.

The Dean's December. New York: Harper & Row, 1982.

"Distractions of a Fiction Writer." In *The Living Novel: A Symposium,* edited by Granville Hicks, pp. 1–20. New York: Macmillan, 1957.

Henderson the Rain King. New York: Viking, 1959.

Herzog. New York: Viking, 1964.

Humboldt's Gift. New York: Viking, 1975.

"An Interview with Myself." *The New Review* 18 (September 1975): 53–56.

The Last Analysis. New York: Viking, 1970.

Mr. Sammler's Planet. New York: Viking, 1970.

Mosby's Memoirs & Other Stories. New York: Viking, 1968.

"The Nobel Lecture." Reprinted in *The American Scholar* 46 (Summer 1977): 316–25.

Seize The Day. New York: Viking, 1956.

"Some Notes on Recent American Fiction." *Encounter* 21 (November 1963): 22–29. Reprinted in *The Novel Today: Writers on Modern Fiction,* edited by Malcolm Bradbury. Manchester and London: Manchester University Press and Fontana, 1977. Totowa, N.J.: Rowman & Littlefield, 1977.

The Victim. New York: Vanguard, 1947.

To Jerusalem and Back: A Personal Account. New York: Viking, 1976.

"The Writer as Moralist." *Atlantic Monthly* 221 (March 1963): 58–62.

2. Other Works

For more comprehensive bibliographical information on Bellow, readers should consult the recently published bibliographies of Francine Lercangée, Marianne Nault, and Robert G. Noreen, listed below.

Aldridge, John W. "The Complacency of *Herzog.*" In *Saul Bellow and the Critics,* edited by Irving Malin, pp. 207–10. New York: New York University Press, 1967.

Atlas, James. *Delmore Schwartz: The Life of An American Poet.* New York: Farrar, Straus & Giroux, 1977.

Alter, Robert. "The Stature of Saul Bellow." *Midstream* (December 1964): 3–15.

Baumbach, Jonathan. "The Double Vision: *The Victim.*" In *The Landscape of Nightmare: Studies in the Contemporary American Novel,* pp. 35–54. New York: New York University Press, 1965.

Berlin, Isaiah. *The Hedgehog and The Fox.* 1953. Reprint. New York: Simon & Schuster, 1966.

Berryman, John. *The Dream Songs.* New York. Farrar, Straus & Giroux, 1969.

———. *The Freedom of the Poet.* New York: Farrar, Straus & Giroux, 1976.

Breit, Harvey. "Talk with Saul Bellow." *New York Times Book Review,* 20 September 1953, p. 22.

Boyers, Robert. *Excursions: Selected Literary Essays.* New York: Kennikat Press, 1977.

Bradbury, Malcolm. "Leaving the Fifties: The Change in Style in American Writing." *Encounter* 45 (July 1975): 40–51.

———. "Saul Bellow and the Naturalist Tradition." *Review of English Literature* 4 (October 1963): 80–92.

———. "Saul Bellow's *Herzog.*" *Critical Quarterly* 7 (Autumn 1965): 268–78.

———. "Saul Bellow's *The Victim.*" *Critical Quarterly* 5 (Summer 1963): 119–28.

———. *Saul Bellow.* London and New York: Methuen, 1982.

Chase, Richard. "The Adventures of Saul Bellow: The Progress of a Novelist." In *Saul Bellow and the Critics,* edited by Irving Malin, pp. 25–38. New York: New York University Press, 1967.

Clayton, John J. *Saul Bellow: In Defense of Man.* Bloomington: Indiana University Press, 1968.

Cohen, Sarah Blacher. *Saul Bellow's Enigmatic Laughter.* Urbana: University of Illinois Press, 1968.

Dommergues, Pierre. *Saul Bellow.* Paris: Grasset, 1967.

Douglas, Mary. *Purity and Danger.* London: Routledge & Kegan Paul, 1966.

Eisinger, Chester E. *Fiction of the Forties.* Chicago: University of Chicago Press, 1963.

Fiedler, Leslie. *Collected Essays.* Vol. 2. New York: Stein & Day, 1971.

———. *Waiting for the End.* 1964. Reprint. New York: Penguin, 1967.

Fisch, Harold. *The Dual Image: The Image of the Jew in English and American Literature.* New York: KTAV Publishing House, 1971.

Freud, Sigmund. *Civilization and Its Discontents.* Translated by James Strachey. 1930. Reprint. New York: Norton, 1961.

Gardner, John. *On Moral Fiction.* New York: Basic Books 1978.

Galloway, David. *The Absurd Hero in American Fiction: Updike, Styron, Bellow, Salinger.* Austin: University of Texas Press, 1966.

———. "Culture Making: The Recent Works of Saul Bellow." In *Saul Bellow and His Work,* edited by Edmond Schraepen, pp. 49–60. Brussels: Free University of Brussels, 1978.

Geismar, Maxwell. "Saul Bellow: Novelist of the Intellectuals." In his *American Moderns: From Rebellion to Conformity,* pp. 210–224. 1958. Reprint. New York: Hill & Wang, 1964.

Glenday, Michael. "'The Consummating Glimpse': *Dangling Man's* Treacherous Reality." *Modern Fiction Studies* 25 (Spring 1979): 139–48.

Gornick, Vivian. "Why do These Men Hate Women? American Writers and Misogyny." *Village Voice,* 6 December 1976, pp. 12–15.

Guerard, Albert J. "Saul Bellow and the Activists: *The Adventures of Augie March.*" *Southern Review* 3 (July 1967): 582–96.

Guttmann, Allen. *The Jewish Writer in America: Assimilation and the Crisis of Identity.* New York: Oxford University Press, 1971.

Harper, Gordon L. "Saul Bellow—The Art of Fiction." In *Writers at Work: The Paris Review Interviews.* Third Series, edited by George Plimpton, pp. 175–96. New York: Viking, 1967.

Harper, Howard. "Saul Bellow." In *Desperate Faith: A Study of Bellow, Salinger, Mailer, Baldwin and Updike,* pp. 7–64. Chapel Hill: University of North Carolina Press, 1967.

Harris, Mark. *Saul Bellow, Drumlin Woodchuck.* Athens: The University of Georgia Press, 1980.

Hassan, Ihab. "Saul Bellow: The Quest and Affirmation of Reality." In his *Radical Innocence: The Contemporary American Novel,* pp. 290–324. 1961. Reprint. New York: Harper & Row, 1966.

Hobson, Laura. "Trade Winds." *Saturday Review of Literature* 36 (22 August 1953): 6.

Howard, Jane. "Mr. Bellow Considers His Planet." *Life,* 3 April 1970, pp. 57–60.

Howe, Irving. "Down and Out in New York and Chicago: Saul Bellow, Professor Herzog and Mr. Sammler." In his *The Critical Point,* pp. 121–36. New York: Delta, 1973.

Josipovici, Gabriel. *"Herzog:* Freedom and Wit." In his *The World and the Book,* pp. 230–244. 1971. Reprint. London: Paladin, 1973.

———. "Saul Bellow." In his *The Lessons of Modernism and Other Essays,* pp. 64–84. London: Macmillan, 1977.

Kermode, Frank. "Herzog." *New Statesman* 69 (5 February 1965): 200–201.

Klein, Marcus. "Saul Bellow." In his *After Alienation,* pp. 33–70. Cleveland, Ohio: World Publishing, 1964.

Lercangée, Francine. *Saul Bellow: A Bibliography of Secondary Sources.* Brussels: Center for American Studies, 1977.

Mailer, Norman. "Some Children of the Goddess." In his *Cannibals and Christians,* pp. 104–30. 1964. Reprint. New York: Delta, 1966.

Malin, Irving. *Jews and Americans.* Carbondale and Edwardsville: Southern Illinois University Press, 1965.

———. *Saul Bellow's Fiction.* Crosscurrents/Modern Critiques Series. Carbondale: Southern Illinois University Press, 1967.

Malin, Irving, ed. *Saul Bellow and the Critics.* New York: New York University Press, 1967.

McCadden, Joseph F. *The Flight From Women in the Fiction of Saul Bellow.* Washington D.C.: University Press of America, 1980.

McConnell, Frank D. *Four Postwar American Novelists: Bellow, Mailer, Barth and Pynchon.* Chicago: University of Chicago Press, 1977.

Morahg, Gilead. "The Art of Dr. Tamkin: Matter and Manner in *Seize The Day." Modern Fiction Studies* 25 (Spring 1979): 103–16.

Nash, Jay, and Ron Offen, "Saul Bellow." *Literary Times,* December 1964, p. 10.

Nault, Marianne. *Saul Bellow: His Works and His Critics; An Annotated International Bibliography.* New York: Garland Publishers, 1977.

Noreen, Robert G. *Saul Bellow: A Reference Guide.* Boston: G. K. Hall, 1978.

Opdahl, Keith. *The Novels of Saul Bellow: An Introduction.* University Park: Pennsylvania State University Press, 1967.

Pearce, Richard. "The Ambiguous Assault of Henderson and Herzog." In *Saul Bellow: A Collection of Critical Essays,* edited by Earl Rovit, pp. 72–80. Englewood Cliffs, N.J.: Prentice-Hall, 1975.

Pearson, Gabriel. "Bellow, Malamud and Jewish Arrival." In *Explorations: An Annual on Jewish Themes,* edited by Murray Mindlin and Chaim Bermant, pp. 18–37. London: Barrie & Rockliff, 1967.

Pinsker, Sanford. "The Psychological Schlemiels of Saul Bellow." In his *The Schlemiel as Metaphor,* pp. 125–57. Carbondale: Southern Illinois University Press, 1971.

Podhoretz, Norman. "The Adventures of Saul Bellow." In his *Doings and Undoings: The Fifties and After in American Writing,* pp. 205–27. New York: Farrar Straus & Giroux, 1964.

Poirier, Richard. "*Herzog,* or *Bellow in Trouble.*" In *Saul Bellow: A Collection of Critical Essays,* edited by Earl Rovit, pp. 81–90. Englewood Cliffs, N.J.: Prentice-Hall, 1975.

Porter, M. Gilbert. *Whence the Power? The Artistry and Humanity of Saul Bellow.* Columbia: University of Missouri Press, 1974.

Rodrigues, Eusebio L. *Quest for the Human: An Exploration of Saul Bellow's Fiction.* East Brunswick, N.J. London & Toronto: Associated University Presses, 1981.

Roth, Philip. "Writing American Fiction." *Commentary* 31 (March 1961): 229–33.

Schechner, Mark. "The Dean's Despair." *Boston Phoenix,* 2 February 1982, p. 2.

Scheer-Schazler, Brigitte. *Saul Bellow.* New York: Federick Ungar, 1972.

Schulz, Max F. "Mr. Bellow's Pedigree, or The Lowered Horizons of *Mr. Sammler's Planet.*" In *Contemporary American-Jewish Literature: Critical Essays,* edited by Irving Malin, pp. 117–33. Bloomington: Indiana University Press, 1973.

Shulman, Robert. "The Style of Bellow's Comedy." *PMLA* 83 (March 1968): 109–17.

Siegel, Ben. "Saul Bellow and Mr. Sammler: Absurd Seekers of High Qualities." In *Saul Bellow: A Collection of Critical Essays,* edited by Earl Rovit, pp. 122–34. Englewood Cliffs, N.J.: Prentice-Hall, 1975.

Solotaroff, Theodore. "Napoleon Street." In his *The Red Hot Vacuum,* pp. 94–102. New York: Atheneum, 1970.

Sullivan, Victoria. "The Battle of the Sexes in Three Bellow Novels." In *Saul Bellow: A Collection of Critical Essays,* edited by Earl Rovit, pp. 101–14. Englewood Cliffs, N.J.: Prentice-Hall, 1975.

Tanner, Tony. *City of Words: American Fiction 1950–1970.* London: Jonathan Cape, 1971.

———. *Saul Bellow.* Edinburgh: Oliver & Boyd, 1965.

Trilling, Lionel. *Sincerity and Authenticity.* London: Oxford University Press, 1972.

Updike, John. "Draping Radiance with a Worn Veil." Review of *Humboldt's Gift* in *The New Yorker,* 15 September 1975, pp. 122, 125–30.

Weiss, Daniel. "Caliban on Prospero: A Psychoanalytic Study on the Novel *Seize The Day,* by Saul Bellow." In *Saul Bellow and the Critics,* edited by Irving Malin, pp. 114–41. New York: New York University Press, 1967.

Wisse, Ruth R. *The Schlemiel as Modern Hero.* Chicago: University of Chicago Press, 1971.

Index

Adler, Dr. (father of Tommy Wilhelm in *Seize the Day*), 37, 96–97, 97–98, 99–100, 101–3; and Humboldt, 167–68; and Tamkin, 96, 104, 106; and Wilhelm's energy, 108; and Wilhelm's need to be loved, 21; and Wilhelm's transcendence, 109–11

Adventures of Augie March, The, 78–80, 94–95; ambivalence toward feelings in, 76–77; and Bellow's task, 25; Chicago setting of, 37, 95, 146; critics' praise of, 78–79; and *Dean's December*, 29–30; father-son conflict in, 118; and *Huck Finn*, 92; and postwar "invisible man," 89; second-half letdown in, 92, 93, 94; and *Seize the Day*, 109; self-definition in, 68; tough-guy nature in, 75. *See also* March, Augie; other characters

Adventures of Huckleberry Finn, The: and *Augie March*, 92

Africa: in *Henderson*, 116–17, 119–21, 146

Allbee, Kirby *(The Victim)*, 53–54; and Dahfu, 125; as "double," 53, 56–57, 58, 64; and Leventhal, 56, 59–60, 61, 62, 64–66, 68, 69, 165, 166; and *Sammler* pickpocket, 148; suicide attempt by, 68

Ambivalence: of Bellow heroes, 14, 23–24, 76, 81–82, 83; in Bellow's attitudes toward America, 76; in Bellow's attitude toward artists, 157; in Bellow's characterization, 96; in *Seize the Day*, 98

America: and Bellow, 24–25, 35, 76, 133, 137–38; *Henderson*'s Africa as, 116, 119–20, 122; Herzog on, 137–38; and Joseph, 51

American Dream, An (Mailer): and Joseph, 48

Artist(s): and Augie, 84–85; and Bellow's heroes, 23; Bellow's view of, 45–46, 157; and Joseph, 45–46, 66; Pearl as, 45

Asphalter, Lucas *(Herzog)*, 18–19, 136–37, 141

Augie. *See* March, Augie

Barth, John, 17

Basteshaw, Hymie *(Augie March)*, 80, 82, 92, 93–94

Beckett, Samuel: Bellow on, 18

Bellow, Saul. *See also* Heroes in Bellow novels

—thought, 13–16, 18–19; on American society, 76, 137–38; and Dostoevski, 13, 14–15; and Freud, 14; and Hemingway, 73, 74; and issues of existence, 41–42; and Joyce, 15–16; and "mind" vs. "experience," 16, 95; and opposite selves, 40; Reich as favorite of, 125; on societal rules, 122; Tanner on, 172 n.4

—works: "afictionality" of, 37, 39, 54, 70; and America, 24–25, 35, 133; authoritarian adults in, 76–77; as autobiographical, 25–26, 32, 35; characters' contradictions in, 163, 164; family in, 86; feelings in, 73; Flaubertian standard of, 70; Gardner on, 54, 70; and *Humboldt's Gift*, 157–58, 171; individuals as subject for, 35–36; "internal mothers" in, 74–75, 76; as life-affirming, 16, 19, 143–44; narrative style of, 174 n.1 (chap. 1), 178 n.1 (chap. 7); "personalities" vs. "minds" in, 54–55;

186

39; and transcendence, 153, 170; virile intellectualism in, 138. *See also* Herzog, Moses; other characters

Hobbes, Thomas: and Joseph, 41

Howe, Irving: on Herzog, 20

Humboldt (Von Humboldt Fleisher) *(Humboldt's Gift)*, 37, 127, 157–58, 163, 167, 168

Humboldt's Gift, 157–59, 162–64, 171; characters' contradictions in, 163; and *Dean's December,* 30–31; and hero's consciousness, 31; thematic tension lost in, 31, 162; tough-guy nature in, 75. *See also* Citrine, Charlie; other characters

Ideas: and Bellow heroes, 20, 22, 31; and Herzog, 132, 138, 141–42

Identity: and Bellow heroes, 22, 25; and Leventhal, 66–68

Internal mothers: in Bellow's men, 74–75, 76

Invisible Man (Ellison): and *Augie March,* 89

Ionesco, Eugène: Bellow on, 18

Itelo, Prince *(Henderson the Rain King),* 117, 121, 122, 125, 126, 128

James, William: and Dahfu's philosophy, 125

Joseph *(Dangling Man),* 39–41, 50–51, 52; and Army, 51, 166; and art, 45–46, 66; and Augie, 79, 82, 83; and autonomy of self, 42–44, 47–49, 50, 65; and brother, 90; concluding search by, 170; as "curbing" self, 123; as "dangling," 19, 39, 41, 47, 51, 52; vs. familial influences, 43, 79; as fearing chaos, 117; and freedom, 19, 42, 47, 48–49, 88; Hemingway attacked by, 73; inner world of, 160; and issues of existence, 41–42; and Leventhal, 53, 59, 61; "old" vs. "new" self of, 40–41, 43, 53, 54; paralysis of, 22–23; and John Pearl, 45; positive values of, 18; and Sammler, 149; violence in, 21, 47, 49, 139; world view of, 44–45, 48, 50, 57, 58, 164

Josipovici, Gabriel: on Bellow, 20

Joyce: and artist's position, 23; and Bellow, 15–16, 18, 78, 95; in *Dangling Man,* 46

Julius. *See* Citrine, Julius

Klein, Marcus: on Bellow's Africa, 120; on Bellow's characters, 173 n.6

Lal, Govinda *(Mr. Sammler's Planet),* 37, 152

Last Analysis, The (Bellow), 14 ⌐

Lausch, Grandma *(The Adventures of Augie March),* 37, 77, 80, 81, 82, 83–84, 85, 86, 92, 94; and Dr. Adler, 103; Augie against, 74; as "hag," 24; nobility lacking in, 127

Leventhal *(The Victim),* 53, 54, 55–56; and Allbee, 56–57, 59–60, 61, 62, 64–66, 68, 69, 165, 166; "angelicism" of, 64; and Augie, 79, 82, 83; "chaos" as threat to, 61, 66, 67, 68; and city life, 107; and complaining, 98; concluding search by, 170; as "curbing" self, 123; as "dangling," 68, 70; vs. familial influence, 79; fears of, 61, 65–66, 67, 117; identity for, 66–68; as inarticulate, 63; intellectual shortcomings of, 54; large size of, 75; repressed rage in, 62–63; sexual impulses of, 61, 64–65; symbolic rebirth of, 68; as "thickened," 55; violence in, 21, 59; world as viewed by, 56–57, 58–59, 60, 61–62

Life magazine: Bellow's interview in, 138

Love: and Augie, 76, 90, 92–93; Bellow heroes' need for, 21, 91; and father-son conflicts, 76; for older brothers, 90; and Wilhelm, 105, 106, 107, 108

Madeleine. *See* Herzog, Madeleine

Mailer, Norman: *An American Dream,* 48; on Bellow, 35–36; as Hemingway progeny, 73; on *Henderson,* 128–29; *Of a Fire on the Moon,* 152

Malin, Irving: on Joseph, 52